10/24

John Pyrl

In Search of John Kyrle
The Man of Ross

Jon Hurley

fineleaf

PUBLISHED BY FINELEAF, ROSS-ON-WYE

www.fineleaf.co.uk

Design: Philip Gray
Typeface: Warnock Pro
Print: SS Media Ltd
FSC Forest Stewardship Council certified paper

Cover: *The Man Of Ross - Distributing Gifts To The Poor* by Joseph van Aken (1709-49)
Courtesy of Hereford Museum & Art Gallery

Published by Fineleaf Editions, 2013
Moss Cottage Studio, Ross-on-Wye HR9 5TB
www.fineleaf.co.uk   books@fineleaf.co.uk

British Library Cataloguing in Publication Data
A catalogue record for this book is available from the British Library.

Acknowledgements

Heather Hurley for her patient guidance in tracking down material. The Revd. Prebendary Andrew Talbot-Ponsonby for a strenuous tour of the belfry of St. Mary's to inspect and photograph Kyrle's Great Bell. Dr. Henry Connor for details of dispensaries in the seventeenth and eighteenth centuries. Elizabeth Semper-O'Keefe and her willing staff at the Hereford Record Office, the Gloucester Record Office, the Hereford Reference Library, and Rosalind Caird, Hereford Cathedral Archives. Peter Darby for examining John Kyrle's Will. P.J. Pikes for information on schools in Herefordshire in the 17th century. Andrew and Heather Jackson for sharing information on their Kyrle memorabilia, including his portrait and an intriguing gold ring, and to Michael Thompson for helping to identify it. Daphne Wyatt for access to previous research on Kyrle. Dr. Fenny Smith for Latin translation. Balliol College, Oxford, for assistance with Kyrle's portrait, Peter Crocker for researching Kyrle's Coat of Arms, to Nick Coleman for a guided tour of the surviving part of the house where Kyrle lived for seven decades, to staff at the Waterworks Museum in Hereford for helpful discussion on wooden 'pipes' used to supply water, and to Philip Gray of Fineleaf Editions, for his designing and editing skills.

A special thanks to the Ross Civic Society for a generous donation from the Richard Shegog Legacy towards the costs of research for this publication.

And what! no monument, inscription, stone!

His race, his form, his name almost unknown!
Who builds a church to God, and not to fame,
Will never mark the marble with his name;

Go, search in there, were to be born and die,
Of rich and poor makes all the history:

Enough, that virtue fill'd the space between;

Prov'd by the ends of being to have been.

Alexander Pope. (1688-1744)

Introduction

John Kyrle was a familiar figure around Ross in the late seventeenth and early eighteenth centuries. He was of medium height with a prominent nose and a cast in his left eye. Most agree he was 'not well read', but a modest, sensible man who cared deeply about the poor. He was a benign eccentric, doffing his tri-cornered hat as he wandered the lanes and byways of his adopted town, nothing escaping his fatherly gaze. He was happiest in old clothes working alongside rustic companions. But it wasn't for this his parents sent him to Oxford and to the Middle Temple to study law.

Kyrle was an enigma, a superstitious, childless, church-going bachelor who visited local schools to berate the children, and sobbed when an extract from the Bible was read. Though a gentleman by birth he inherited no mansion, or white railing'd paddock where hunters grazed. He was High Sheriff of Herefordshire, a post then reserved for well bred gentlemen. Distaste for pomp put him off holding high office for life.

It was said that Kyrle had neither the ambition nor the intellect to make a barrister and politician like his father. Not caring what his wealthy relatives thought, he sallied forth daily, marching across Ross with his quartet of laughing labourers by his side, his sleeves rolled, a spade on his shoulder, a flagon of home brewed cider in his pocket and a bundle of cuttings under his arm. When in the company of his loyal helpers, the Man of Ross's childish humour and playfulness was exemplified by a ring he wore, 'which on touching emitted the head of a hissing snake'.

Kyrle inherited a modest house overlooking the town centre, which he extended. He was a man of simple tastes, but nobody's fool. He lived with his cousin, Judith Bubb, and various retainers. He was self-sufficient and liked his own company. He retired early most nights, usually after a visit to St. Mary's Church to pray, perhaps pausing on the way home to visit one of a cluster of inns a short walk from his front door, to quaff a jug of cider and chat with his neighbours, regardless of their social standing.

After the chastening deaths of both parents when he was still in his twenties, Kyrle returned to Ross to try to establish himself and build a career. With family contacts and friends in the Church, Kyrle embarked on several important projects to improve the town and benefit its citizens. He led the team that rebuilt a causeway battered for centuries by severe floods that swept pedestrians, carts and animals to their deaths. The new causeway made Ross accessible and returned the town to economic independence.

Kyrle helped bring fresh water to Ross by having it pumped through hollowed out elm logs. He rented the Prospect, the loftiest, handsomest, perch above the Wye, so that the poor and raggedy could sniff roses and roll their hoops on gravelled paths.

A devout Christian, Kyrle helped replace fallen pinnacles and mend the broken spire above St.Mary Church. He handed out bread to the starving as they gathered in rags, their bony hands outstretched, on the icy steps of the Market Hall. He dispensed potions and pills to the poor. With Miss Bubb by his side, he visited the sick in their squalid tenements. He brought comfort to the dying, helped to arrange their funerals and prayed at their gravesides. He traipsed the town in all weathers, calling on the aged in their almshouses, seeing that they were comfortable and fed.

John Kyrle was 87 when he died 'full of years'. He had accomplished enough for the poor of his adopted town to merit the cognomen, the Man of Ross. It was said his contributions to Ross on a daily basis, 'sanctified it from the boisterous vulgarities' of most provincial towns. As he lay on his death bed, Kyrle's affection for Ross and its poor was undiminished. The poor mourned him, drawing tattered shades and kneeling in prayer. He was interred under the chancel floor, his demise recorded 'by the good Vicar Prince' with this simple entry in the Ross Parish Records, 'in handwriting double the size of any other', '1724, Nov. 20th. John Kyrle buried'. After all he achieved for Ross there was no monument to mark the great benefactor's final resting place, no bronze in the Prospect, no pigeon-stained statue in the market place. After three hundred years of indifference, it is time to go in search of the forgotten, and elusive, John Kyrle, the Man of Ross.

Pedigree and Coat of Arms

According to John Kyrle's own 'very accurate and methodical' family history, he owed his existence to Robert Crul, an ambitious foreigner who slipped into England from Flanders, a bloodstained conundrum of a place scattered around parts of Belgium, France and Holland. In sight of British shores, Crul changed his name, not for the last time, and figuratively tore up his passport. By 1295, now called Curl, he found employment and soon rose to be a bailiff tied to a farm belonging to the Bishop's Manor of Ross. He was given a scrap of 'apportioned land, subject to a range of agricultural services and fines'. Curl had security of tenure and could not be transferred to another place or owner.

Now spelling his name with an 'e', Curle sent for his mother, wife, and children and worked with admirable application, until 'by a solemn deed of 1302 he was manumitted to the Bishop'. Making a gigantic leap, Robert Curle or Curl, is believed to have lived for a while at Altone, or Old Town, now Alton Court, Ross before moving to Homme, now Hom Green. For his loyalty and diligence, and now called Robert Crul of Hamme, 'with Matilda, his wife, and all his offspring begotten and to be begotten, together with all his goods, holden and to be holden, he was rendered forever free, at a cost of forty marks, and quitted from all yolk of servitude'. This energetic, fiercely ambitious and intelligent individual was 'the common ancestor' of the Kyrles of Walford Court and the Clarkes of the Hulle. The house still stands but is now called Old Hill Court, and is described as a circa 1600, timber framed, Grade 2-listed building.

William Curl, son of Robert, had 'numerous progeny'. By intermarrying with the Pyes, Markeys, Scudamores, Lechmeres, Herefords and Abrahalls, the cream of Herefordshire society, the Curls mopped up genes and land until their heirs rose from serfdom to sipping vintage port with the rich and powerful. It took four centuries but the persistent Cruls, Crylls, Curls, Kyrls, Kirles and finally, Kyrles were English gentry at last.

The next adornment had to be a Coat of Arms, with a short and memorable motto, preferably in Latin. The Kyrle Coat of Arms is plain and modest, featuring a gold chevron between three golden fleurs-de-lis, against an emerald background, with a golden hedgehog for a crest on a green mount. The motto selected was *nil moror ictus*, (I do not care for blows); a crescent was later added to the shield. The hedgehog symbol dated back to the Doomsday Book, when Archenfield, an area close to Ross, and lying between the Rivers Wye and Monnow, was known as Arcenfelde, the 'felde or land of the hedgehog'. The cautious creature also appears on the heraldic arms of the Abrahalls of Foy. John Abrahall's arms boasts three hedgehogs, one more than Kyrle. In defiance of Kyrle's adoption of the hedgehog, the following ditty appeared.

Now stands of Kyrle the crest;
And thrice of shield of Abrahall
The urchin's form impressed!

'The hedgehog', Gwillim wrote, 'signifieth a man expert in gathering of substance, and one that provident layeth hold upon proffered opportunity, and making hay whilst the sun doth shine'. The hedgehog, slow moving, shy, cautious, wary of intruders, with a body 'armed like a phalanx', was depicted on the shield to intimate that 'the bearer was ready to answer any attack from his antagonists'. It is possible that Kyrle's hedgehog briefly gained official recognition, becoming the emblem of the town until 1951. Ross Urban District Council applied in 1952 for their own Coat of Arms, which was granted in 1953.

Often alone in his rambling old house, with its low beamed ceilings and heavily curtained windows, confinement for Kyrle must have been very irksome for one so active. To kill time he wandered his echoing rooms, mallet and gimlet in hand. Like a schoolboy obsessed with gouging his name on his desk, the Man of Ross disfigured several doors by crudely inflicting on them in nails his coat of arms, date of birth and hedgehog motif.

John Kyrle arrived via a quartet of Walter Kyrles, beginning with the gentleman of that name who was born in 1489 and lived in the Hill in Walford. The line trickled down to a second Walter of Walford Court, whose son, Robert begat John Kyrle's father, the Oxford educated Walter Kyrle. John Kyrle's father married Alice, daughter and sole heiress of John Mallet of Berkeley, who was previously married to Walter Carwardine, a Barrister of Carwardine Green in Herefordshire.

John Kyrle's grandfather, James Kyrle, of Walford Court, was High Sheriff of Herefordshire in 1629. He married Anne, daughter of Robert Waller of Beaconsfield, sister of the colourful Edmund, a poet and politician who was arrested for his part in a plot to establish London as a stronghold of the King. Waller saved his neck by paying a £10,000 bribe and betraying his fellow conspirators. The Kyrles would prove to be no strangers to deceit and betrayal. Thomas Kyrle of Walford, a scion of a family which would produce, 'two such eminent but widely discordant members as John Kyrle, the loyal Man of Ross, and his kinsman, the rebel Colonel Robert Kyrle, one of Cromwell's most active officers', purchased a portion of a manor in Much Marcle once owned by the mighty Mortimers.

John Kyrle's father entered Oriel College, Oxford, on April 11th, 1617, aged 17, and was called to the bar at the Middle Temple in 1625. He practiced as a Barrister of Law on the Oxford Circuit, was a Justice of the Peace, and MP for Leominster in the Short Parliament, having won the seat in April, 1640. He was again successful seven months later, winning the Leominster seat in the Long Parliament, and holding it until 1648 when he was excluded under Pride's Purge.

The velvet stranglehold prominent landowners had on parliament is shown by the way the Hereford seat, since the early seventeenth century, was passed like a juicy plum from one member of an unelected cabal to another, with powerful names like Scudamore, Hoskyns, Westfaling, Foley, Walwyn, Hopton, Cornewall, nodded through without the tedium of canvassing, ballot boxes, and vote counting. A soft handshake and a knowing smile sufficed.

Gloucester Born

John Kyrle was born on the 22nd of May, 1637 in the White House, Dymock, Gloucestershire, a property his father inherited from his wife's family, and one where, during the Civil War, Sir John Winter maintained a troop of horse, and lived there after he deliberately burned White Cross House, Lydney in 1646 to prevent it falling to the Roundheads. The advowson of the church of Dymock, rented in 1548 for 40 shillings, which passed to the Winters and then to the Humphreys, consisted of the White House estate, rectory and vicarage. After the Dissolution of the Abbeys in 1539 the advowson finally passed to Edward Wilmot who leased it to William Winter of Lydney. The legality of Winter's tenure was doubtful so the title was granted in 1615 to Sir Edward Winter of Lydney and his brother William Winter of Coleford. In 1616 Sir Edward released all his rights in Dymock to William Winter of Coleford who made the presentation of the new vicars in 1626, 1654 and 1664; John Kyrle acted as patron in 1678 'for this turn'. But, we are getting slightly ahead of ourselves -back to Kyrle in his cradle.

The infant Kyrle was baptised on the 4th of June in the Church of St. Mary the Virgin, a grey edifice across the road from where he lived. The long demolished White House had a lane on the north side leading to a wood where young John Kyrle ambled alone, instilling in him a stubborn self reliance and an appreciation of nature. The Kyrles had two other children, Walter, who was 'born an ideot', and a daughter Sybil, of whom little is known. The Rev. Charles J. Robinson, author of a History of the Mansions and Manors of Herefordshire, claims Walter, 'who was unknown to fame', was alive in 1683. No trace of the man has been found.

When given John Kyrle's pedigree by Mrs. Clarke of the Hill, Charles Heath, a Monmouth bookseller, thrice Mayor of Monmouth and author of *Excursion Down the Wye*, said it was extraordinary that he could not obtain any information about Kyrle's handicapped brother Walter, 'either with respect to his residence, marriage, death, or any other circumstances whatever'. Heath wondered if young Walter's conduct 'had sunk him amongst the mass of mankind, or that he left the kingdom at an early period of his life'. Kyrle's brother, it seems, was expunged from the record, probably out of shame. He was subsequently restored, appearing in a hand written family tree, amended and checked by the Rev. Richard Kyrle, Vicar of Walford.

Dymock was prosperous and of some renown. Rural and tranquil, the population was educated and comfortably off. Robert Burhill who worked with Sir Walter Raleigh on his History of the World was born here in 1572. The snug village boasted properties dating from the 15th century, including copyhold cottages described as burgages. It remains an attractive place with 71 listed buildings, the Church of St. Mary and the Cider House at Grade 1. The imposing High House, which still stands, was once the home of a former London vintner, John Perton of Lime House.

Dymock's main harvests in Kyrle's time were the 'golden fleece', the finest wool in Europe, and apples. Flourishing orchards were in abundance, their blossoming described by Rudder, as 'a garden overspread with flowers, words prove inadequate to describe the beauty of this flowery landscape'.

In 1645, the eight year old John Kyrle might have heard from an open window the distant boom of cannon heralding the ominous advance of the Civil War. In Ross, King Charles I (1600-1649) is said to have dallied in Gabriel Hill's Great Inn, on the corner of Church Street. If only young John Kyrle, an embryonic Royalist, who would become enthralled by stories of the King's son, could had been there to joyously flutter the royal colours. Less welcome visitors tramped across Gloucestershire.

Under the command of the Earl of Leven, starving Scots mercenaries bullied their way into Herefordshire. Then, 'with ravenous rapacity', their bloodstained pikes visible above the hedgerows, they raided outlying hamlets, included Dymock, sacking it to the tune of £1,104.11s.4d. Ross citizens, their businesses barely recovered after the plague, hardly deserved to be poked and threatened by braided buffoons, who lolled about the town, eyeing the pretty girls and keeping the inn keepers happy. The mercenaries who boasted they 'could endure all heates and colds, march with a weeks provision of porridge', drove off stolen cattle to slaughter and devour.

John Kyrle's father was an 'adherent of both sides', and played a minor role in the Civil War. In a letter dated July, 1646 to William Scudamore of Ballingham, he detailed the way the local commanding officer, Harry Lingen, should peacefully and with humanity, evacuate Goodrich Castle, after a battle that left the castle a glowing ruin and the air heavy with the stench of cremated flesh.

'Sir Henry Lingen', Walter Kyrle wrote, 'hath ended the business according to our presage at Hereford, he and his Souldiers are to march forth this day att of the clock, leaving all things behind them butt what they carry in theyr pockets, they are to deliver up theyr armes att the Oulde Gore and continue all prisoners to the Governour at his pleasure, the Collonel here present presents his service to yr selfe my good Cosen and the like is really done by, Yr faithful Kinsman and Servant, Wat Kyrle. Ross ult. July, 1646'.

Young John Kyrle meanwhile, trotted to the local school where it is believed that he was taught by Edward Reese, a highly respected schoolmaster, whom history places on a list of Dymock's men of distinction. Kyrle was later enrolled at Gloucester Grammar, a school intended for young gentlemen. Less affluent parents criticised Grammar schools 'for the narrowness of a system which taught Latin and nothing else to boys ignorant of their mother tongue'.

The Kyrles eventually left Dymock, exchanging the certainties of rural tranquillity for bustling Ross on Wye ten miles away. While, far away in a London street, King Charles I, 'a man of blood', nibbled a piece of bread and drank a glass of claret before walking unsteadily through a spitting rabble to his place of execution. After a rambling speech, the repentant monarch expressed a determination to die a Christian according to the profession of the Church of England. He laid his neck on the block, 'and after a little pawse', the Executioner at one blow, severed his head from his body, and held it aloft to jeers.

Arrival in Ross

Camden described Ross as a market and free borough town made by King Henry the Third, in Greytree hundred. It was stoutly built, populous, and well-frequented by reason of its markets on Thursdays, which were 'plentifully stored with cattle and other provisions'. Markets were also on Ascension Day, Corpus Christi, and St. Margaret's and St. Andrew's days. According to the Reverend T.D. Fosbroke, Ross did 'not resemble country towns in general, the houses being various, and the shops frequently showy. This relief enlivens the streets', he wrote.

To Walter Kyrle the meandering approach to Ross was familiar. This 'younger son of a family of lesser gentry, (who) had little land of his own', is reputed to have built the house in the Market Place in 1620; and used the address when he was admitted to the Middle Temple in 1625. The timber framed building was stone built, on the slope of a hill in a narrow street. It was later considerably extended, boasting fifty feet of frontage, projecting stories, carved timbers and small-paned windows, comprising bedrooms, parlour, buttery, kitchen and study, 'with a space left in the rear wall to accommodate a timber-framed rear wing'. The garden would be enlarged by a plot of land purchased from another stout Christian, Toby Fecknam.

In Ross, the plague was still painfully fresh in the memory. Stories were told of deserted houses, inns and shops, their curtains flapping as the owners fled. Quacks hurried from the Market Place. St. Mary's Church was padlocked against the needy and the terrified. The Rector, a silk scarf to his nose, bolted, his eyes swivelling. Only John Price MA, a poor but devout preacher with few adherents, worked through the night as corpses piled around them. After the last cadaver was interred, the pits limed and the sod drawn over the staring dead like a quilt, the hollow eyed Price, defiant and filthy, led what remained of his flock in a tar lit procession through the echoing town. Three hundred and fifteen of the four hundred and fourteen nameless souls who died in 1637 are remembered by a stone cross, lichened and leaning in Ross graveyard. The heroic Price is not commemorated anywhere, in wood, stone or stained glass.

In the Saracen's Head, across the road from the Kyrle's house, with its 'carved Tudor roses, heads with pointed beards and moustaches, and foliage and grapes on the beam beneath the eaves', vintner John Farne pottered among his weeping casks, the air redolent with the pong of spilt wine. Farne was fondly remembered for 'succouring his aged vicar the Reverend Price, when he was cruelly evicted from his living'. Unlike the saintly Price, Farne has a memorial in St. Mary's -a grinning death's head and a cherub, with the inscription 'Neere ys place lyeth ye body of John Farne, who was generally beloved and faithful to his friends, and who departed ys life in ye true faith of Christ, May 24th, 1658'.

Compared with sleepy Dymock, Ross was a vigorously poked anthill. It was lively, noisy and smelly. Men bought and sold. Sheep and swine waited patiently to be slaughtered. Dogs gnawed bones flung by bloodstained butchers, and cats perched on sills, their tails twitching, watching rats evade the boots of laughing labourers. Drunks tumbled from fly buzzing inns. The Kyrles had settled into a life in Ross befitting minor gentry; they kept to themselves and entertained at home. Walter Kyrle's sudden death on February 10th, 1650 came as a great shock to his wife and son. Richard Stallard, bailiff for Ross Borough for the year 1648, reported delivering his accounts for 1649 and 1650 to Mr. Walter Kyrle, 'about three weeks before his death'. Kyrle was fifty years of age. John who had finished grammar school was seventeen.

The Kyrles were not well off. When a hearth tax was levied on houses at a cost of two shillings per hearth, collectable in two instalments on Lady Day and Michaelmas, John's widowed mother was asked to pay 18 shillings a year. A contribution to the Hereford Militia Assessment was also levelled according to the ability of the householder to pay. While she paid £8 to Rosse Burrough and £1 to Rosse Forren in 1665, Robert Kyrle living in opulent Walford, paid £200, the highest in the district.

Life in Ross was improving with efforts made by town officials to attend to litter, collect pig, horse and cattle droppings, and after the weekly market, sluice blood, feathers and guts from outside the butchers. Signs were put up in the town. 'We demand that all the inhabitants of Rosse, that bringe Mucke, sile or dunnge to the Markett house or Markett place, that they carrie it away or cause to be Carried away weekly in pyne of 7/8 pence a peece'.

Wardens, 'officials of the manor court', patrolled the town looking for violations and visiting houses to warn of fire hazards. Margery Endell had been ordered 'not to make fyer in her house where there is no chimney'. William Mann was castigated for the 'annoyance of his pigges', which he hand fed from his door, allowing them to nuzzle titbits off the cobbles, then snooze, ears twitching, in the shade. Citizens were obliged to 'ringe and yoke their pigges'. Several who didn't were fined one shilling and six pence per animal. One genteel widow, whose house overlooked the 'Markett place', was required to remove 'the soyl and rubidg under her stone wall att harterslane end'. The culprit was identified as Mrs. Kyrle, John's mother. Years later, John Kyrle himself, was 'presented at court for not removing a dung-heap in front of his dwelling house'.

When the market traders deserted the place for the day, the space was used for entertainment. From a window the teenage John Kyrle, with time to kill while he prepared for Oxford, might have observed apprehensive bulls arrive in creeled carts, lowing and tossing their heads in fear and frustration as mischievous urchins poked them with sticks, and terriers leapt and snarled, dying to sink their teeth into the monster's dung smeared hide.

Off to Oxford

Alice Kyrle was determined that John should follow his late father to Oxford, then to the Inner Temple. She entered her son for Balliol in 1654. A law degree was seen by ambitious parents as a gilded gateway to success and influence. Balliol, a college noted for its liberal tendencies, had roots going back to Lord John de Balliol, who, for insulting the Bishop of Durham in 1226, was publicly whipped outside the cathedral and ordered 'to start a school in a small house outside Oxford city walls, where poor children would be educated for pennies'.

From this unlikely beginning, Balliol prospered, becoming one of the largest colleges of the University of Oxford, with diverse alumni that included, a King of the Scots, Adam Smith, author of the Wealth of Nations, writers John Dryden, Robert Southey, Aldous Huxley, Gerald Manley Hopkins, Robert Browning, Graham Greene, and Algernon Swinburne. Politicians include Herbert Asquith, William Gladstone, Lord Curzon, Viceroy to India, Lord Beveridge and Boris Johnson.

By the early 1650s, the Civil War had drained the college coffers. Silver reserves were melted in a hastily erected mint in New Hall to produce currency. The town was occupied by Parliamentarians who put to the sword those who backed the wrong side, demolished the castle and levelled defensive earthworks. Upon being accepted as a Gentlemen Commoner, on April 21st, 1654, John Kyrle was expected to pay 'caution money' in the form of silver.

As the driver shook the reins in the Ross Market place, and the stage coach rattled down Old Gloucester Road, Kyrle, a reflective boy who had rarely ventured beyond the green fields and woods around Dymock and Ross , firmly held his suitcase and hugged his silver tankard. He was bound to be excited, and more than a little apprehensive. Of his contemporaries, few swotted for degrees, preferring to opt for a 'gentlemen's degree', in drinking, gambling and hooliganism.

The future Man of Ross was leaving the town as religious tension flared with the arrival of Quakers in Brookend Street. A number of them were arrested on their way to a prayer meeting at Kings Caple, an unwarranted incident that resulted in one innocent dissident being clamped in the stocks and pelted. Friends' meetings were often disrupted 'by a Rabble with Dogs, whooping, haloeing, pushing their Staves in at Windows, and throwing Dirt'. Mobs stalked Quakers, 'striking one of them, Giles Milton, so violently he became lame in one of his arms'. In another incident John Merrick, a mild mannered Ross tanner and generous benefactor, 'was beaten and sorely abused by a servant of Walter Kyrle, for failing to doff his hat to certain gentry'.

Oxford was beautiful, vibrant, broke and unable to pay even household bills. Balliol was obliged to 'lend' the King £210. To achieve this, officials had to hand over all its precious domestic plate, then valued at £334, for melting. The loan was never repaid. When the Royalists reclaimed power, the intellectual life of the University was soon fermenting. Lubricated by mountain madeira, and headed by the likes of Sir Christopher Wren, debate of the highest order led to the founding of the Royal Society.

There were bookshops with buckled walls, heavy books and beams, and a multiplicity of dimly lit taverns where students clutched jugs of ale, befriended maidens and argued. Delectable aromas swirled from bakeries and coffee houses. Everywhere the stone was warm and honey coloured, even in the back streets, where craftsmen worked in wood, leather, paper, cloth, glass and paper. On sunny pavements students mingled with tourists. Oxford's fame as one of the world's most eminent seats of learning had become a tourist attraction which contributed substantially to the economy of the town.

Kyrle strolled the tranquil quad, where a gnarled mulberry tree, planted by Elizabeth 1 still pushes out green shoots and radiant blossom.

The Old Library, where Kyrle read cross-legged, was built in the 15th century and still functions. Kyrle presented Balliol with the solid silver tankard hallmarked 1669-70, and cast by Thomas Jenkins, a London Silversmith. It weighed a fraction under nineteen ounces and inscribed, 'ex dono Johannis Kyrle de Rosse in agro Herefordiensi'. Revealing unexpected brio, the future Man of Ross promised that should any student offer better, 'he would enlarge his gift'.

Young Kyrle heard some happy news. In a will dated August 15th, 1670, John Winter, mariner, son of Margaret Wintour of Dymock, 'being in perfect health and memory, blessed be God for it, left his uncle John Kyrle, the silver plate and ye three pieces of gold that remaines in his hands'. Winter also left 'old Gamer (grandma) Cole of Dimmock the sume of £3, if she be dead my desire is that it should be distributed to the poore people of Dimmock'.

Kyrle entered the Middle Temple in 1657, but abandoned his studies and returned to Ross around the time of the Restoration. On the 25th of May, 1600, an event momentous to Kyrle, occurred. His hero Charles II landed at Dover and was rushed to London to be crowned. From a feverish, flag waving London crowd, John Evelyn watched the King emerge from his carriage, 'his way, straw'd with flowers, the bells ringing, the streetes hung with Tapissry, fountaines running with wine: the Major, Aldermen, all the Companies, in their liveries, Chaines of Gold, & banners; Lords & nobles, Cloth of silver, gold & vellvet everybody clad in; the windows & balconies all set with Ladyes, Trumpets, Trumpets, Musick'.

Royalist Herefordshire rejoiced. The citizens of Ross capered and sang. 'Upon Wednesday, being the happy day of His Majesties' birth, as well as his and the Common Prayer Book's restoration, the most considerable persons in Ross thought it not enough to celebrate the day with praise and prayer, as well as sermon, but to express their inward joy of heart the better, they caused a face of wood to be cut, which being dressed with a long mantle and a cape, with solemn league and covenant upon his breast, was carried on a pole by a chimney –sweeper (instead of a hangman) dressed in his holy day apparel, that is, as black as he could be; two of the same quality carried up his train, and in this triumphant manner after evening prayer he was solemnly carried quite through the town, the drummer and guard of musketeers besides the pike men attending him, till at last he was brought to the market-place, fixed to the ground, the covenant having the inscription -

> *Who set three kingdoms in a flame?*
> *Tis just, should perish by the same*

And so burned to ashes with acclamations of great joy not easily to be paralleled...and all this to show their affections to His Majesty and the Ecclesiastical Government under which they and their ancestors lived so happily, to God's glory and their own comfort.'

It is not known for certain if John Kyrle observed either the choreographed London celebration, or the disorganised but heartfelt knees-up in the Market Place in Ross. The flamboyant, manipulative, womanising Charles, who enjoyed the fragrant charms of at least fifteen mistresses, including the Hereford associated ingénue, Nell Gwynne, greatly appealed to the smitten Kyrle. Delighted with the new King's victory, but aware of his diverse family's political affiliations, Kyrle may have felt a twinge of remorse on behalf of his relatives. If he did, it didn't stop him having a logogram dedicated to the newly crowned King, consisting of an F and a C intertwined with a heart, roughly meaning 'Faithful to Charles in Heart', carved in stone. Kyrle had the love symbol inserted in a cleft in the Market House. This was apparently because he could not gaze upon the bust of his hero which had been fixed to a gable end of the Market House, and was invisible from his window. Kyrle's joy was short lived. On March 24th, 1662, his mother died.

An inventory dated April 3rd, 1663, lists the interesting contents of the house Kyrle inherited. They included over £40 worth of gold plus 'linnen wheele, turkie cushions, olde chaires covered with Cloth, joyned stooles and stooles covered with leather, a fether bedde, a straw bed, a flocke bedde, a bedsteede with curtains, a truckle bedde, boulsters, twelve flaxen sheets, old holland sheets, olde worne hurden sheets, and pillow beeres, eight dozen trenchers, andirons, a payre of tongues, brass potts, panns, posnetts and basons, chaffing dishes, skimers, a cullender, a Cisterne, three chamber potts, over forty items of pewter, including candlestickes. In the kitchen there were 'spitts, olde iron drippings pans, pott hookes, a fire shoule and' a fish pike. The 'sellar' bulged with four 'hoggsheads of syder, one of home brewed beer, a barrel of the same, a brewing skeele, a brewing fate and eleven empty hoggsheads & firkins'. In 'ye Backside and Stable' nestled 'two small piggs for fattening, wood and coles, one Nagge and an olde saddle and packsaddle'. The total value of the contents of the Kyrle's house was under £200. They owed £235 borrowed by bond.

Kyrle kept his word, and in 1670 gave his college a second tankard - a silver monster weighing sixty-one ounces, which is still in use at the college. The tankard is eight inches high, stands on three stubby solid silver legs, each featuring a dolphin and a cover lifted by Kyrle's crest, a large, silver hedgehog. It holds five pints of liquor. The lid is engraved with the Balliol arms and in the centre of the body is the Kyrle's family crest and inscribed underneath, *Pocculum Charitatis, Ex dono Johannis Kyrle, de Rosse, in agro Herefordiens et hujus collegeii socio commensalis*, (The gift of John Kyrle of Ross, in the county of Hereford, Gentleman Commoner of this Society).

The tankard was placed under the care of the Butler to the College who produced it when 'any gentleman from Herefordshire honoured the Society with their company'. Charles Heath was at Oxford, endeavouring 'to collect the floating memoirs of a character (John Kyrle) whose name will be handed down the stream of time as long as the English language continues either to be known or to be spoken'. As he perused the inscription on the Kyrle's tankard, Heath said that the engraver was 'guilty of a great omission, by neglecting to insert the date of the year the tankard was presented'. Heath missed an opportunity to toast Kyrle: the Monmouth man had already drunk too deeply from the university's famous cellars when the Butler invited him to take one last swig from the Man of

Ross's tankard, 'so that we might offer to the good Man's Name one faithful draft'. Though 'nothing could exceed the kindness of the officer to whom it was intrusted', Heath was reluctantly obliged 'to decline a favour I should otherwise have proudly accepted'.

Amenities in Ross were improving. Financed by Frances Duchess of Somerset, whose family held the Lordship of the Manor, the Market House was built opposite Kyrle's house, between 1660 and 1674. Samuel Ireland called it 'a ponderous and unmeaning heap of stone'. Insults notwithstanding, the gnarled and weathered old red sandstone building, one of the few buildings of note in Ross, has been in constant use ever since. It once served as the Manor Court, comprising a steward to the Lord of the Manor and town officials, who met on the top floor three times a year. Many of the cases heard concerned the selling of stale products, loose and unruly animals, safety regulations and road repairs. Most were minor charges punishable by a warning or a small fine. For more serious offences, miscreants were put in the stocks. Public flogging was practiced in Ross, as was the occasional use of the ducking, or 'cuckynge' stool, when women were plunged into the Wye, often for scolding lazy husbands. When the Ross ducking stool disappeared, the Manor court demanded its immediate return. The stool was not only for women, but also for men 'who in the course of their trade sold short measures, adulterated food, or were caught brawling in public places'. The last public ducking in Herefordshire occurred in Leominster in 1809, with Jenny Pipes, as the final victim.

Kyrle was in demand. Margaret Wintour, of Dimmock (sic), in her will dated September 22nd, 1674, left gold, diamond, pearls and property to a host of relatives, not forgetting, 'the poore of the parish of Dimmock', to whom she gave 'the sume off forty shillings to be disposed of according to the discretion of my executors'. Mrs. Wintour 'desired her well beloved friends, her in law, Mr. John Kyrle, and Mr. Bridges, 'to see this my last Will and Testament accomplished and performed whence I doe make and appoint overseers of the same'.

Looking to Religion

Both parents dead, Kyrle was without a friend, money, or a means of earning a living. At this low point in his life, he derived emotional strength from his religion. He became a daily visitor to St. Mary's Church, a familiar solitary figure kneeling alone in a matrix of empty pews. Friends he made among influential clergy would be key to his building a reputation as a diplomat and facilitator of the great projects for which he would later became known. As a young man returning to Ross after several years away, Kyrle would have to tread warily, careful not to get the wrong side of a cloistered cadre who could do him good or ill.

He became acquainted with the fascinating Reverend John Newton, MA, (1621-1678), a man of 'distinguished talents in the higher branches of science'. Newton was a Commoner at St. Edmund Hall, Oxford in 1637, obtaining a BA in 1641 and an MA in 1642. A Royalist at the Restoration, in 1661 he was made King's chaplain and rector of Ross. Observing the deplorable state of local education, Newton informed wealthy landowners that Ross lacked two things, 'a comfortable subsistence for God's ministers, and a competent endowment for a good school'. A zealous pamphleteer, in 1668 he published 'The Scale of Interest or the Use of Decimal Fractions and Table of Logarithms, for the use of an English, mathematical and grammar school to be set up at Ross'.

Newton was somewhat older than Kyrle, entering Oxford the year Kyrle was born. He was never seen out of his gown, brewed his own ale and erratically trimmed his beard. He was whimsical and musical. He wandered the fields at night gazing at the stars. He measured spires and trees, kept a chest of tools in his study, composed his own sermons and delivered them with passion.

Unlike Kyrle, Newton was a liberal in church matters, looking kindly on 'free-thinking Christians' and supporting Quakers, whom he encouraged to remain within the Church of England. Below is an extract from his tongue-in-cheek eulogy, translated from the Latin:

Within this holy place, beneath a simple stone, sequestered in the darkness of the grave, lies he, who, living, gained through learning's orb, a never-dying fame!...Earth, with all her honours, could afford but a tribute of applause to the divine utility of his labours,-in the bosom of his God alone is their reward.

In Business

Kyrle quickly established useful contacts in Ross and its environs, using the family name to galvanise support. Visits were made, hands were shaken, strings pulled. In doublet, frock coat, breeches, hose, buckled shoes and wig, Kyrle set to work. The first proof is a deed dated September 27th, 1666, between himself and Sir William Powell of Pengethly. The document reveals that Kyrle purchased from Powell a messuage and diverse parcels of land, meadow ground, and a key purchase, the pasture in Ross known as Cleeve-field Bank, an unfenced strip stretching ' for nearly a mile along the brow of land commanding so many and so changing views'. Kyrle later 'tastily hung' the slope with elms. The resultant small forest became known as 'Little Wood' and featured on the third line in Pope's Eulogium. It was a promising start, the first of a lifetime of enjoyable and rewarding wheeling and dealing as Kyrle developed his property, consulting and conveyancing interests, carrying on until the grave beckoned many years into the future. Kyrle's conscience was untroubled by the fact that Sir William was on the opposite side in the Civil War.

Kyrle proved to be a man of substance, and would soon be acknowledged as a trusted and fair-minded negotiator, with fingers in many a juicy pie. He soon became a trusted middle man when the gentry were looking for one of their own, someone discreet, and cheap, who would work all hours designing arcane inheritance routes to keep and increase their fortunes. In tandem with William Gwillym Snr. of Langstone, Kyrle organised a complicated 99 years lease on Walford Court, as well as other land and properties in Walford, for wealthy spinster Elizabeth Kyrle. In 1689, with Sir Edward Harley, of Brampton Castle, Sir William Merrick and other senior gentry, Kyrle witnessed Articles of Marriage for Robert Yate of Bristol, which included complicated lease and release clauses, covenants and an alternative plan in the event of a default of male issue. He was involved in the sale 'Low Copp, also Hope's Land, and Brommy Close in the lordship of Wilton under Wye to Thomas Shough of Tretire'. He owned property in Gloucestershire, as well as in and around Ross. His name was coupled with John Hereford's as a trustee of an estate upon the marriage of John Maylords of Hereford, Gent., to Penelope Hereford, spinster. After a shaky and unpromising start, Kyrle's career took off.

By taking on rickety barns and tumbledown messuages in Bridstow, Peterstow, Walford, as well as Dymock, Berkeley, (the latter held with Lord Berkeley), and several other parishes in Gloucestershire, Kyrle was able to built a useful property portfolio for himself. The properties involved were often nothing more than ivy wrapped ruins, nettle-covered paddocks or leaning tenements. Nothing was too dilapidated for Kyrle, who always saw its potential.

He began inviting interested parties to his house to discuss letting, renting and selling. He offered small cash advances to those who desired a better house, on condition that he supervised the design and the building. So in demand did he become as agent, planner, architect and mortgage broker that 'no gentleman would fix on any plan before it had received the approbation of Mr. Kyrle'. Possibly because he lacked framed diplomas on his walls, Kyrle didn't overcharge for his services. One idealistic chronicler wrote that Kyrle gave his services free, 'his taste gratified, without any expense'. Not quite, Kyrle knew his worth.

He was now an eligible bachelor. Sadly there is no evidence of the rustle of tulle as carriages drawn by shiny geldings passed through the iron gates of country houses after gay and colourful balls.

Balliol College library portrait (courtesy University of Oxford) ———

Nor was there the merest glimpse of a feverish and scented love letter. On the face of it Kyrle seemed too bound up in himself, his many faceted interests and his God, to commit to a partner. His greatest pleasure seemed to be in attending church, sometimes twice a day. In the evenings, 'at the chiming of the bells, all business ceased with him. He closed his ledgers, washed his hands and retired'. Or, he visited the Nag's Head with its capacious wine cellar and curved exterior wall, making it easy for carts and coaches to glide past. From stables at the rear, the vinegary scent of horses wafted. Kyrle's heavy oak chair, highly ornamented, polished and dusted, stood awaiting the great man as he arrived for his evening libation. His association with the Nag's Head led to the formation of the John Kyrle Lodge of Loyal and Independent Old Friends. Kyrle distributed his custom evenly, for at the New Inn, now the Eagle, appropriately on the corner of Kyrle Street, the Loyal Man of Ross Lodge, Manchester Unity was founded. Both Lodges came into existence in 1853, long after Kyrle had departed.

Settling Disputes

John Kyrle enjoyed playing the role of peacemaker between warring neighbours, be they poor or prominent. Thomas Hearne (1678-1735) wrote: 'When any litigious suits fell out, he would always stop them going to law'. Kyrle, who 'made it a mission in life to arbitrate in a local quarrel' was regularly engaged as a wise and independent arbiter by the poor, who appreciated his diplomatic skills in re-examining old and divisive disagreements, skilfully easing them towards satisfactory conclusions without involving lawyers, who he seems to have despised. His reputation as an unbiased broker meant Kyrle was invited to umpire an apparently intractable dispute between Ross Town and Ross Forren regarding the equitable paying of taxes. A tribute to his maturity and deft touch. Kyrle opened and closed the debate with a religious flourish:

Seventeenth century summer house, Homme House, Much Marcle ———

To all Christian People to whom this present writing shall
come, I, John Kyrle of Rosse in the County of Hereford Gent,
send greeting in the Lord God Everlasting. Whereas by an order
under the Hands and seals of Herbert Westfaling, Rudhall
Gwillym and John Nourse, Esq. Three of His Majestie's Justices
of the Peace, for the sd County, bearing date the Two and
Twentieth day of September, One Thousand Six hundred and
Twenty Three, the Controversy between the Town and Forreign
of Ross, Touching the Inequality of their taxes was referred to
Richd. Clarke and John Bennett, on behalf of the Forreign and
to Richd. Furney and Richd. Harris, on behalf of the sd Towne
to settle the same by a General survey of both; in case they
should faile to Compose thereby that the then sd Difference
Should be determined, the sd John Kyrle as Umpire and
Indifferently chosen between the sd P(ar)ties.

After tortuous legal exchanges an agreement was finally reached, enabling Kyrle to sum up.

For ye Future all manner of Taxes w(ha)tsoever to be Imposed
upon the sd Parish of Ross shall be p(or)p(o)rtioned between the
said Town and Forreign as Eight is to Thirteen. Also that the
Forren shall reimburse the Town what they have Pd the Poor
more than the p (ro) p (or) tion since Easter last.... I the SD Jno
(sic) Kyrle, with the Consent of the arbritators, do order and
declare that the Money raisd by the Assessmt as aforesd shall
be distributed to the Poor indifferently as they shall have need.
And also what rents or Money have been or shall be given by
any Charitable persons to the sd poor. In witness the sd John
Kyrle and we the said Arbritators, Richd Clarke, Jno Bennett,
Richd Furney and Richd Harris as concenting to this Order,
have hereunto sett our Hands and seals this Twenty Eight day
of October, Anno Dni, 1674.

Letter circa 1694 co-signed by John Kyrle (Hereford Record Office) ———

Noverint universi per presentes Nos Johannem Kirke groc de
Ross in Com Hereford, Arild ffrumfraw Jones groc & Wm Johannis
Raste in Civit Hereford etc, et Georgium Kill do o adem groc
nayler

teneri et firmiter obligari Reverendo in Christo patri ac Dno Dno
Gilberto ... die ... in ... Liter b bona et legalibus mone-
te Angl solvend eidem Reverendo in Christo patri aut Suo certo Attor-
nato Successoribus his Assignariis suis ad que quidem
solucionem bene et fideliter faciend obligamus & quemlibet
libet nrum per se pro toto et in solido ... & heres et execut
nros firmiter per presentes Sigillis nris Sigillat Dat quarto
die mensis ffebruarij Anno Dni 1694 ...

The Condicion of this obligacon is Such That if the above bounden John
Kirke the Administrator of the goods Cattles and Chattles of Mris Mary Chubb
the late wife of Jeremiah Chubb &ct whilst shee lived of this ...
County of Hereford deced during the minority and nonage by ...
to make or Cause to be made a true & perfect Inventory of all Singular the goods Chattles
Creditts of the sd deced which have or shall come to the hands ...
knowledge of him the said John Kirke ... or into the hands possion
of any other person or persons for him & the same so made do exhibit or Cause
to be exhibited into the Regy of the Consistory Court of the dioces of Hereford
at or before the fourth ... day of May next ensuing the same
goods Chattles & Creditts & all other the sd goods Chattles & Creditts of the sd deced at
the time of the death which at any time after shall come to the hands & possion
of the sd John Kirke ... or into the hands & possion of any other person or persons
for him do well & truly administ according to Law & further do make or Cause to
be made a true & just Account of his sd Adicon at or before the thirteenth
Day of January next And all the rest & residue of the sd goods Chattles & Credits
which shall be found remaining upon the sd Administrators ... Account
the same being first examined & allowed by the Judge or Judges for the time
being of the said Court Shall Deliver & pay unto Such person or persons
respectively at the sd Judge or Judges by his or their Decree or Sentance
pursuant to the true Intent & meaning of a late Act of Parliament in
that behalfe made & povided Shall limit & appoint, & if it shall hereafter
appear that any last Will & Testament was made by the Deced & the
... or ... therein named do exhibitt the same into the said Court making
request to have it allowed & approved accordingly If the sd John Kirke
above bounden being therein to required do render & Deliver the sd Lettrs
of Adcon Approbacon of Such Testant being first had & made in the sd
Court Then this obligacon to be void & of none effect or els to be in full
forme Effect & Virtue

Sigillat et Deliberat in presentia nrum

Jam: Hoods ...

John Kyrke

Ricardi Pyer

ffrances Jones

George Kill

Kyrle also negotiated a deal with traders using the Ross market to contribute the sum of 56 shillings and 8 pence per annum to destitutes in Rudhall's cottage hospital. Howard Erskine–Hill, author of *The Social Milieu of Alexander Pope*, states 'It is clear that (Kyrle) was able to profit from his years at the Middle Temple in advising his fellow townspeople about their practical affairs and in acquiring the reputation as a man knowledgeable in the law. Kyrle's work for the poor of Ross was largely unpaid'.

Kyrle continued to pick up small legacies from dead relatives, and offers of gainful employment, sometimes simultaneously. In his will dated September 16th, 1681, Giles Wintour, grocer, a relative living in the parish of St. Sepulchre's without Newgate, London 'being sick and weak in body but of sound and perfect mind and memory, bequeath unto my uncle John Kyrle Esquire, the sume of £10 of lawfull money of England to buy him mourning'. Wintour also left his uncle 'the sume of £20 of lawfull money being other part of the said legacie intended for my said child as token of the respect I to him (bear) for his great --- and kindness in my education and bringing upp. And I doe hereby disire and appoint my said uncle John Kyrle and my said late Master Mr Elidad Blackwell, to be overseers of this my last Will and Testament disiring them to be ayding and assisting to my said executrix in the execution thereof'.

Kyrle was also prepared to intervene objectively if an employer, in this case a friend, appeared to be treating a tenant unfairly. On November 8th, 1703 he wrote to important landowner J. Walwyn, Esq., regarding Thomas Hopkins, whom Kyrle learned had fallen behind in his rent. Hopkins's daughter had called upon the Man of Ross seeking advice, using the excuse that her father was 'busie a sowing',

Kyrle informed his friend Walwyn that Hopkins 'was very sensible of his owing you a good deal of rent, but ever since the cheapness of corn he has fallen behind, but promised to clear the Lady-day rent by Christmas, and the Michalmas rent before the next

St. Mary's Ross (extract) by William Farror, 1832 ———

Lady-day'. Mr. Roberts, who appears to be an employee of Walwyn's and responsible for collecting rent, had been exerting pressure on Hopkins to pay, even though Hopkins had already paid £40 on account and could find no more.

'I lately spoak w'th Mr. Roberts', Kyrle wrote, 'who sees that your fine will be perfected by ye end of this term'. Kyrle said Hopkins would find it difficult to keep his promise and suggested he should be allowed to clear two small orchards and to plant trees to supplement his income. He asked Walwyn if he knew of any workmen 'in ye neighbourhood who were expert in planting', If not, Kyrle said, he could supply men who, 'know very well how to digg and set trees', and promised 'to travel over to Longworth, eight miles distant, on Friday, unless something falls out to prevent it'. In which case he would travel, 'on Saturday next in ye evening, if ye weather proves favourable'. Kyrle ended on a friendly note. 'Our maid Frances lyes very ill, and 'tis feared will not recover. My best service to yr brother and all ye ladies, I rest, Your friend and Servant, John Kyrle.'

The dispute was settled amicably, with no loss of face on either side. Erskine-Hill commented that 'of the fourteen deeds of Kyrle's which I have been able to examine; only three concern his private interests'. Life for Kyrle was sweet; his bank account was healthy and his address book full of important contacts.

Rebuilding the Causeway

Confident in his own ability, the ambitious Kyrle began looking for a cause that would both benefit his fellow citizens and raise his own profile in the town. He was familiar with the seasonal problem of flooding near Wilton Bridge, when the turbulent Wye swamped the area, cutting off the town. It was a problem that required a determined visionary to solve. Kyrle, 'whose mind seemed ever

Sketch of Kyrle's Causeway, John Hall, 1827 (Jackson Collection)
Surviving arches from Kyrle's Causeway

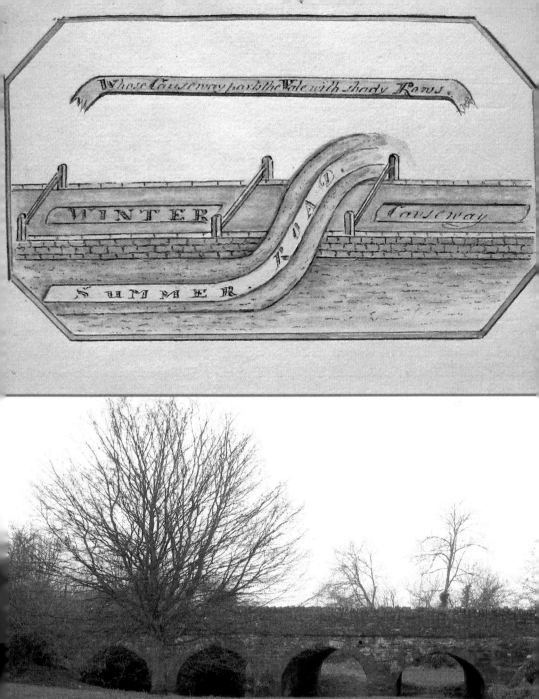

awake to promote the public interest, until doing something became an object of public attention', called a meeting with potential backers and Church officials. Lively argument and earnest pleading ensued. Kyrle's calmness and non-judgemental personality engendered a feeling within his peers that a complicated and expensive project that would help the town and make money, a problem that went back in time, was, with the help of God, not insurmountable. The Herculean effort 'Kyrle employed to fund the building of the causeway to Wilton Bridge', cannot be over estimated. It was one of his greatest triumphs.

Stratford was among those who wondered how the Man of Ross was able to achieve so much on an income of just five hundred a year, the rent he obtained from his properties. The answer was that Kyrle did not pay for the work. He was a well connected facilitator, who was comfortable cajoling and chivvying his rich friends to open their chequebooks. Dr. Johnson (1709-1784) commented succinctly that 'Kyrle was a man of known integrity and active benevolence, by whose solicitations the wealthy were persuaded to pay contributions to his charitable schemes: this influence he obtained by an example of liberality, exerted to the utmost extent of his power, and was thus enabled to give more than he had.'

The diplomatic but stubborn Kyrle used all his energy and conviction to drive the project over, through, and past the many obstacles that were put in its way. Through powerful and imaginative friends, some of whom were known benefactors, funds to excavate the site were secured. It was a monstrous task by hand. The rutted route had to be raised by at least eight feet. Teams of navvies, stone masons and volunteers worked long and wearying hours. The result, according to an article in the Gentleman's Magazine in 1753, was 'a noble causey leading up to the town, 923 yards long and 14, and in some places 18 feet wide'. Kyrle spent months at the scene, encouraging the workforce and making sure contributions procured by him continued to replenish the coffers, until a long and handsome causeway was open to traffic. The stately avenues of elm saplings Kyrle had planted on either side 'gave the traveller a very fair prejudice' of the sandstone town on the hill. The new trees thrived and would soon grew stout and tall all the way up to the entrance of Ross as if it were Rome or Athens.

The causeway was an immediate success, 'promoting the business of the town and ensuring the safety of its users, human and animal'. The completion of the project was commemorated by a pillar bearing the legend, 'At this spot was cheerfully begun what is now happily completed, the labour of this Causeway, winding in the parishes of Ross and Bridstow, hence to the Black Pool bridge, and thence in a connected line to the Lady Pool arch'. Kyrle added a personal note: 'Thus traveller having regarded thy ease, we bid thee speed well on they journey in the good name of God'. The completion of the vital link, also re-uniting Ross with the important towns of Monmouth and Hereford, was another of Kyrle's finest achievements, and 'a monument of his zeal for promoting the interest and safety of the public at large'.

It was essential to keep the causeway regularly maintained and safe from flooding. From 1726, Hereford and Ross combined to form a Turnpike Trust, which maintained the route over Wilton Bridge and the causeway. It was used by an assortment of horse drawn vehicles including chariots, landaus, and berlins, together with stage and mail coaches. Waggons loaded with stone, timber, lime and corn were hauled uphill by teams of horses or oxen. Pack horses carried coal from the Forest of Dean; cows, sheep and geese plodded to Ross market. It says much for the design and skilled workmanship involved, that in spite of the rapid and weighty increase in usage, the causeway survived many turbulent winters. While disparagingly described as either 'in need of repair', 'greatly out of repair', or simply 'ruinous', Kyrle's causeway was kept functioning with an occasional expenditure of a few pounds, the largest being £74 in 1780. By 1799 the fine shady rows of elms that Kyrle planted had 'long bowed their heads to the axe'. The pillar which proudly commemorated the opening of the causeway disappeared in 1827. Sadly, almost nihilistic vandalism seemed to shadow Kyrle for most of his life.

The Prospect

Gazing out on the crouching tenements that almost clung to his home, Kyrle noticed how many poor children's noses were glued to dirty and cracked window panes. Like damaged butterflies they were trapped in fetid prisons, without the sight of a flower, a bird, even a scrap of green. Kyrle was determined to do something about it. He seized an opportunity to become involved after the passing of the Dowager Duchess of Somerset in 1692, for whom Sir James Kyrle of Walford Court was an attorney and steward.

When the lordship of the manor of Ross fell to the Right Honourable Thomas Lord Weymouth in 1693, Kyrle accepted an offer to lease from Weymouth several properties and tracts of land. They included the Old Mill, and two parcels of meadow lying between the mill and the Great and little Reakes, also the meadows known as Lincolns adjoining the Aylemarsh, as well as a piece of arable land called Hall's Croft. Also, on October 1st, 1693, Weymouth, with whom Kyrle clearly gelled, wrote to him offering to lease 'all that piece or parcel of Arable Land commonly called or known by the name of the Bishops' Court'. The level upper ground, that appeared in William Fisher's will in 1709 as the Prospect, was destined to retain that name.

Weymouth teasingly added a coda: Kyrle had to take three keys and 'keep in repair, the three towers', a reference perhaps to the towers that survived the demolition of the Bishop's Palace. It was an astute move by Kyrle, who by signing a lease for 500 years, secured for the town 'a free place of resort which would ever be a delight and attraction to all frequenting this eminence'. Kyrle was not simply accumulating land as a mere investment. His plan was to plant trees and 'raise fine grass plotts therein and other ornaments as he should devise to make the same a free walking place for the Inhabitants of Ross and all other persons who would resort here for their diversion'.

He sub-let four acres of ground to Fisher, an ambitious Quaker, for 495 years at £5 a year, payable half yearly, but retained the right 'to work the land as he saw fit', digging ditches, erecting such buildings, and other ornaments he thought fit to make it a public walking place. Kyrle wanted liberty for all to have free ingress and egress to and from the said land called Bishop's Court land, even allowing the 'whitening and drying of Linen clothes upon grass plots and hedges without leave or license or of paying any recompense or reward whatever'.

Covenants were signed to 'preserve all trees, plants and grass plots, not to molest or hinder the said John Kyrle or his workmen in building walls, levelling ground, or any other matter whatsoever'. The lease forbade Fisher from 'erecting any building, stanks, stack, rocks, privy house, pigs cot, stalls, or pens for pigs or plant any hedges, or do any matter or thing that may annoy or incommode or be a nuisance to the said Walks or the Prospect or pleasantness thereof. Nor to turn or suffer to be turned in, Beasts, or Swine into Bishop's Court, but graze some with sheep, the soil or dung of such sheep to be spread thereon. To weed the grass until it be made clean and free from weeds. To mow down the grass which by the staining of said Sheep shall be standing higher than other parts thereof. To keep the walks well cleansed and in all respects preserve the Walks and the rows of trees and all other ornaments the said John Kyrle placed there'.

Kyrle successfully completed the landscaping and building of the Prospect by 1700, topping it off with a spectacular and ornate fountain. A figure stood in the middle of an eight feet deep oval bowl, which held five hundred and fifty hogsheads of clean water, spraying all and sundry all day long. In the winter it froze and during the summer children played in its refreshing arc. The fountain was an extravagance which Kyrle felt the poor, who had very little of that commodity, would appreciate and enjoy. Besides, the excess water was delivered to the town via pipes and stopcocks for everyone, thus eliminating the need to haul basins and buckets to and from scattered springs and wells.

'With a small, but well-chosen, piece of ground', Erskine-Hill wrote, 'Kyrle had created a major piece of landscape-gardening'. With the fine architecture of the gateways (and probably the fountain) it must have been expensive in time as well as money to a man of his small fortune. But his achievement was a fine one which he dedicated with goodwill, dignity and grace to the public. In this achievement Kyrle was not modest and self-effacing. His name and arms adorned the sundial in a niche in the west wall of the Prospect. His cipher was on the pediment of the south and north gates. As he made clear in his will, Kyrle wanted recognition. He desired that his name 'should be perpetuated'.

Kyrle's public gardens, created after many years of fund raising and voluntary labour, worked well for seventeen years until in consideration of a one off payment of a further paltry five pounds by Fisher, by deed of a letter dated November 24th, 1713, Kyrle rescinded many of the covenants of the lease. Disastrously this allowed Fisher 'to turn in and depasture beasts and pigs ringed'. As the pig and cattle market was attached to Fisher's inn, weekly deliveries of animals to the market were allowed to mill around the land that Fisher controlled, turning the it into a foul porridge. It was a rare error of judgement by the normally cautious Man of Ross which had dire consequences.

The dispute between the citizens who regarded the Prospect as theirs, given to them by the then late Man of Ross, and James Barrett, a no-nonsense entrepreneur, who bought the Pounds around 1837, and with it Kyrle's lease to Fisher, would rumble on for years. Barrett levelled the Pound Inn and upon its site erected the Royal Hotel, illegally enclosing part of the Prospect 'for the future and exclusive use' of those staying at the Royal'. Barrett fenced off part of the old Bishop's Court at the rear of the hotel and had his gardeners refresh limp rose beds and replant jaded shrubberies. By stealth, he turned the Prospect into an exclusive garden with lawns and pleasure grounds, widening and extending the path from the churchyard to facilitate his visitors.

Barrett's gardeners did a fine job. There was neatness and order where there once was muck and inky pools, the rockeries were repaired and replanted, leaning and lichened trees were felled and replaced by healthy saplings. The part of the Prospect 'stolen' by Barrett was beautiful, but it was private and no longer available to the citizens of the town for whom it was intended by Kyrle. Enraged vandals, joining mild protesters, snapped Barrett's young trees, played football with uprooted plants and prowled the Prospect perimeters, frightening the hotel's gentle clientele, swearing and generally making a nuisance of themselves. Barrett responded by building a solid stone wall around the land he had acquired, erecting signs declaring the ground 'Not Public' and chaining newly hung gates. The hotelier's action led to serious and lengthy outbreaks of lawlessness.

An urgent meeting of the inhabitants of the town of Ross, and its neighbourhood, was convened for December 3rd, 1839, at the Town Hall 'for the purpose of considering the steps necessary to be taken to maintain and preserve the rights of the Public over the Prospect, threatened to be extinguished by Mr. Barrett, the Proprietor of the Royal Hotel, in the town'. The first resolution, moved by Mr. Joseph Edwards, and seconded by Mr. Thomas Cooke, on John Kyrle's 'philanthropic design of dedicating the Prospect to the Inhabitants of Ross, and all other persons resorting to the Town, who might be disposed to avail themselves of it as a free walking place', was unanimously passed. A second resolution, moved by Dr. Underwood and seconded by Mr. John Purchase, on 'the conduct of Mr. Barrett, in having erected a board in the Prospect, with a notice upon it, declaring the ground Not Public, and seeking to exclude the public altogether from it, was unwarrantable and arbitrary, and not only unjust but a gross insult to the immortal Man of Ross, as defeating that object, which is a well authenticated fact, was one of the warmest wishes of his heart', was unanimously supported. Barrett refused to yield to the wishes of the townspeople and their lawyers, James Wallace Richard Hall and Messsrs Edwards, who volunteered to conduct the necessary legal measures without any professional profit'. The fight for justice continued with an uneasy peace tested by regular disturbances.

Upon Barrett's death the Royal passed to Thomas Roper, a family dentist and chemist, in 1857. Roper was a fellow Town Commissioner of Thomas Blake's. They became close friends. It was from Roper that Blake purchased the Royal Hotel and grounds, including the Prospect. The riots continued. On Monday July 12th, 1869, there was a major disturbance. A crowd, in a cider induced state, gathered. They were joined by ale swigging members of the erroneously named Barrel Friendly Society, who had been celebrating their anniversary by triumphantly marching behind the Trafalgar band, thumping drums and blowing brass instruments. Wound up belligerents attacked the town's billiard-room, snapping cues and using billiard balls as missiles. One drunk clambered onto the green baize in muddy boots and attempted to deliver an address but fell off.

Soon after 6 o'clock the wholesale destruction of the Royal Hotel gardens commenced. Peas, beans and cabbages were ripped from the soft soil and trampled underfoot. Roses were uprooted, flowerbeds desecrated. Soil and shattered earthenware littered the paths. The crash of greenhouse glass upped the tempo. Someone suggested lighting a fire. Bean sticks and other inflammable articles were piled up near a dry hedge next to one of John Kyrle's gates, and set ablaze. Axes were called for to splinter wooden fences. Willing hands fed the leaping flames, which now crackled the length of the Prospect, causing the black and gold paint on Kyrle's gate to blister. Water-butts were reduced to staves and thrust into the fire, which blazed in a dozen separate places, reducing everything in its path to ashes.

Looting and yelping went on till midnight when the sleeping Royal Hotel was attacked. Stones smashed windows and landed on beds and bounced off polished furniture. The riot raged until a timely squall sent sooty faced revellers back to both tenements, and to large houses, for it turned out that some of the protesters were eminent citizens, including Mr. James, a surgeon, Mr. Powell, a chemist and Mr. Powle a prominent local businessman.

The Ross Gazette reported that 'during the time the destruction was going on, the police, though near at hand, remained aloof for their own safety'. The following day a posse of constables, armed with cutlasses, were despatched from Hereford and stationed around the Prospect, offering no molestation towards the townspeople who continued to moodily roam the Prospect at will. The following evening, speeches were delivered, all bearing on the right of the people to the Prospect. Some mouthed Pope's eulogy to the man of Ross. But this was not a solemn, Kyrle-led, family outing with everyone holding aloft peace signs. The riot was full blown, resulting in severe injuries and bloodletting.

When grim faced Town Commissioners walked the battered and dishevelled Prospect to inspect the smouldering shrubs and broken walls, they decided to hold a special meeting on July 16th, 1870 to settle the matter once and for all. In the midst of all the wise nodding and agreeing, Thomas Blake, a nationally known dissident preacher of the sort Kyrle would not have approved, discreetly purchased the freehold of the 'best and largest' part of the Prospect, with all the rights thereunto belonging, for £100, and presented it to the citizens of Ross, by deed, for their use forever. It was a wonderful and fitting ending to a dispute that lasted well over a hundred rancorous years. Ross celebrated. And if Kyrle's massive bell didn't joyously pound that day, and if the 27 inns of the town did not run dry, they should have, for it was a memorable day in the history of Ross.

Slaking the Town's Thirst

The gentry once took their water from lakes, wells and springs on their own land. The poor used springs too but they were often isolated and foul, requiring a backbreaking walk for a woman or a child, often uphill on the return, with two heavy and slopping buckets which threatened to separate their hands from their wrists. In earlier times the Bishops had their own supply. The remains of a medieval well belonging to the Bishop's Palace that was discovered and destroyed by the building of the Wilton Road in the 1830s confirms this.

Recognising Ross's dire need for easily accessible fresh water, Kyrle arranged with William Fisher and three other Ross men in 1705 to take over the sixteenth century One Mill and Rix Meadows which Lord Weymouth had leased to Kyrle eight years before. The Rudhall Brook, a forceful stream at the bottom of the town, was channelled into a narrow leat that flowed through the meadows by the Rope Walk, curving right to the waterwheel at Ross Dock. Wye water was piped from here up to a reservoir on the Prospect, using elm trees that had been cut into ten or twelve-foot lengths, split into two halves, hollowed out and the two halves bound tight together to make a pipe. Water was conveyed from the reservoir to 'public cocks in the town'. Such an arrangement had its limitations and the supply was often disrupted, especially in winter when the water froze solid in the pipes, causing them to burst. Kyrle's fountain became a receptacle for litter, leaves and dead animals. Money and time were spent to little purpose.

In 1713 the waterworks changed hands. Finance was secured, the blocked pipes were discarded and iron pipes were introduced. The new company continued to pump water to a reservoir sunk under the Prospect. The refurbished fountain gushed once more but it didn't last.

A further attempt to supply water to the town was made in the mid-eighteenth century by John Puckmore, who rented a meadow from Guy's Hospital, intending to 'reserve to himself a liberty of laying pipes, thro' which he would serve the town of Ross with water'. Although Puckmore paid rent to Guy's in 1754, there is no evidence he ever pumped water to the town. Later benefactors continued to try to solve Ross's perennial water problem. In 1818 Joseph Turnock, who had moved to Merrivale with his sister, was soon excavating a reservoir, building a pumping station and aiming to supply the whole of Ross with limpid water. The mission failed due to 'many difficulties', resulting in the Merrivale Water Works being some way short of the success anticipated.

Enter again Thomas Blake, who examined the possibility of extracting water from deep artesian wells he had dug on land purchased above the town. Controlling the water supply, be it a village spring, well, town pump, or impressive waterworks, is a licence to print money; we can see that by our relentlessly increasing water bills. Blake's scheme led to the establishment of the Alton Court Water Works, solely owned by him, in 1887. Blake built a reservoir 'as big as a ballroom', with a capacity of 10,000 gallons, 'under the wide pathway in the churchyard near the entrance from St. Mary's Street'. Eighteen eighty-nine, the date he finished the project is fancily etched into the stone steps leading up to the churchyard from Palace Pound. Benefactors are seldom content to be anonymous. Blake's water, constantly replenished from his artesian wells, was pumped throughout the town, thus enabling Ross's other great benefactor to finish what John Kyrle started.

Declined Company

Kyrle, a slightly eccentric bachelor who spent too much of his time mixing with the poor and the pious, a man who had little time for soirees and who rode a furry cob, was unlikely to appeal to his smooth, socially superior, relatives. As a young man with plenty to prove, he 'declined company'. But as he mellowed, Kyrle was 'exceedingly pleased if his neighbours dropped in without ceremony, when he made a good long evening of it, enjoyed a merry story, and always seemed sorry when it was time to break up'. Thomas Hearne wrote that 'his only vice was he tooke two pipes of tobacco a day, either at home or elsewhere'. It is pleasing to know the worthy Man of Ross had at least one vice.

Kyrle 'dinnered' close friends, regardless of their status. They made a point of calling on the Man of Ross on Thursday, market day, occasionally 'forming a very large circle, where personal worth and humble merit, were more attended to than dignity or fortune'. Kyrle was superstitious and never dined with an even number. It had to nine, eleven, or thirteen, including himself and Judith Bubb. Neither fancy food nor drink appeared on these occasions. Instead, the table was spread with plain food which guests ate without ceremony.

His expenses being trifling, Kyrle 'was therefore able to lay by for the poor, a greater portion of his income than most men have inclination or the self denial to give up.'

Close to his kitchen fire, Kyrle kept a bench of rough oak where the poor sat while Miss Bubb sliced a cheap beef cut she'd stewed, serving it on slices of freshly baked loaves. While meat was plentiful, and relatively inexpensive, except for venison which was considered the height of luxury, Kyrle ate little of it most of the year, except on important occasions when a joint of beef was roasted and served with potatoes, peas, beans and artichokes accompanied by cider. If guests preferred wine, Kyrle kept a small cask of it, also one of a 'malt liquor'. But cider was his personal favourite. It was a known antiseptic and 'an extensive branch of the wealth of the county'. Kyrle's belief in the health-giving properties may have been justified. In this he had much in common with John Evelyn (1620-1706), whose motto was *omnia explorate; meliora retinite*, 'explore everything, keep the best'. Like Kyrle, Evelyn went to Balliol College, enjoyed designing pleasure gardens, and loved 'strong and pleasant cider, which excited and cleansed the Stomach, strengthened Digestion, and infallibly freed the Kidnies and Bladder from breeding Gravel Stone'. Both seem to prove the efficacy of cider drinking. Evelyn died at 86 years of age, with Kyrle pipping him by a year.

Kyrle was also known to enjoy roast goose. Compared to beef, it was rare and expensive, with more than one bird required to satisfy a large gathering. Kyrle was a self-styled master of carving and when doing so he revelled in the performance. An anecdote in Brand's Popular Antiquities refers to the intricate business of carving a creature that is almost all bone. Brand asserted that when carving a goose one should hit the joint with venom while thinking of a cuckold. Thomas Webb, carver to a Lord Mayor of London in the reign of Charles I was both an Olympian cuckold and deft carver. Kyrle displayed rare humour when carving, bellowing 'Hold your hand man: if I am good for anything, it is for hitting a cuckold's joints'. The names of various local persons were put forward as potential cuckolds. Though much laughter ensued, no guest would dare to attempt to relieve Kyrle of his greasy knife. For dessert, plum pudding was often served, but also a kind of seventeenth century spotted dick, made from milk, eggs, sugar, suet, raisins and marrow.

When the servants had dined, what remained of dinner was gathered up and given to the poor who shuffled hopefully past Kyrle's door. In winter, while rich Ross landowners retired to London to escape 'dreary prospects and clouded skies', Kyrle remained at home 'diffusing the comforts of food, fuel, raiment, and attendance, among the sick, the indigent and the old'. For the remainder of the year there was a tougher side to the Man of Ross, who expected everyone who applied to him for relief to be prepared to do something for themselves 'as far as was consistent with age and health'. He considered it 'a tax upon, diligence and industry, to support any but the aged and infirm: doing otherwise would encourage indolence and inactivity'. A constant source of menial employment for the active poor was therefore provided by Kyrle at a daily rate. This often meant gathering stones, way mending, clearing woods, and other small tasks, adapted to the strength and abilities of his various supplicants.'

High Sheriff

In 1683, Kyrle, aged 46, colourfully robed and tasselled, followed five relatives into the post of High Sheriff of Herefordshire. Dating from the 11th century, it was the oldest secular office under the Crown, quietly passing from one gentleman to the next in line. By accepting the honour, Kyrle joined the ranks of the top Herefordshire families, the Chaundos, Walwayns, Devereuxs, Scudamores, de la Mares, Baskervilles, Crofts, Mortimers, Lingens, Vaughans, Bodenhams, Harleys, and the Rudhalls. Although Kyrle was on the Commission of the Peace for several years, 'he seldom or never', sat on the Bench. One bauble was enough for the modest Kyrle, who declined all other offers, including that of Justice of the Peace, although the role 'gave a justice important social standing'. Instead of spending many tedious hours dealing with humdrum affairs, having to mix with JPs who varied 'from the casual and lazy' to the annoyingly energetic and conscientious, Kyrle took the opportunity to groom his nag and set off to visit friends in South Oxfordshire.

While riding near Benson, 'a royal centre of great importance', a dusty and fatigued Kyrle was arrested. Constables were on the lookout for suspicious looking strangers after a series of burglaries in the area. The arrival of a dishevelled and irritated Kyrle fitted the bill. Vigorously protesting his innocence, the Man of Ross was taken in for questioning. But, the instance his name 'was made known to the magistracy, neighbouring gentlemen hurried in their carriages, to bail him'. A beaming Kyrle thanked his friends, mounted his moulting old nag and trotted down the winding and dusty dirt track that many hours and stops later, would take him back to Ross.

Kyrle received the sad news of the death of King Charles on February 6th, 1685. The king's fatal illness occurred on February 2nd, Nell Gwynn's thirty-fifth birthday. John Evelyn confirmed that his Majesty's last utterance was 'that Nelly might not starve'. It is hard to gauge how much the passing of the lively and colourful King effected Kyrle. It is bound to have made him, without a wife, children, partner or close friend, feel suddenly mortal. And around the corner lurked a totally unforeseen event that would cost the Man of Ross countless sleepless nights. He was, unwittingly, about to become father.

Children

How did John Kyrle, a staid, middle-aged bachelor with little experience of children or of the opposite sex, come to have two young girls, Elizabeth and Judith Bubb, foisted upon him? From copies of letters Kyrle wrote it would appear that he 'fostered' the children when their feckless father deserted the family. They were the offspring of Colonel Jerimiah Bubb, Usher to his Majesty King William, and his wife Mary, formerly an Abrahall. Elizabeth, the older child by nine years was baptised on November 11th, 1679 at Foy, Judith followed in April, 1688. Their father, 'a man of great parts', lived life to the full, 'extravagantly spending in expectation of further advances in his profession as a soldier'.

Bubb's cavalier behaviour seems to have left the family destitute. Matters worsened. The Colonel had an aunt in Hampton, Gloucestershire, a Madam Tooke, who had a son Buck, by a former marriage. One day when the Colonel was absent in London' Buck turned up at Ingestone, Herefordshire. Spinning a yarn, he glibly wheedled £120 from Mary Bubb. As a result of this deception, one account melodramatically related, 'poverty came upon the lender, and in a little while, death'. Mary Bubb did indeed die, on the 19th of May, 1689, a year after giving birth to Judith. She was buried in Foy graveyard, her still legible tomb bearing the recumbent effigy of a priest, together with the Bubb coat of Arms - an azure with three urchins survives in Foy graveyard. With the constantly wandering Colonel absent on another of his mysterious jaunts, Elizabeth and Judith were facing an uncertain future.

Kyrle, a cousin with a large, practically empty house in Ross, was prevailed upon to receive the girls, probably on a temporary basis. Though hardly happy about the intrusion, he accepted the girls into his home, with all the chaos associated with displaced children. Assisted by his servants, Kyrle fed, clothed and entertained the waifs. He endured the experience and the cost for a while before writing to Madam Tooke, requesting the return of the £120 her son 'borrowed'.

Initially, the money was paid by irregular instalments. When that dried up, Kyrle wrote again, on February 6th, 1701, referring to the distress caused by the persistent non-payment of the balance, which 'to my knowledge, caused some unkindnesses between husband and wife, because they wanted it themselves, being not in a position to lend money and now the condition of their children is very low, which causes me to petition you on their behalf. The letter continues:

Of this £120, your son hath payd £86 and there is now behind
of the bond besides interest of £34, to which I formerly writ
to him about, but had no answer, and for some yeares since I
understand he removed from Hampton. I know not whither
which causes me to write to you, his mother, (knowing you to
be a worthy conscientious, person of good ability), desiring and
hoping that you will take the condition of these poor children
into your consideration, so that they have their money,
which will be a great kindness to them, as if it 'twer given to
them; hoping to have a favourable answer from you, I rest,
Madam, Yo humble servant t com'and, John Kyrle, Ross, in
Herefordshire, this February 6th 1701.

Kyrle added a postscript:

Your neeces here gives their duty to you. I forgot to let you know
that I had the happiness formerly to be known to you, being
sometime in your hows, when Colonel Kyrle was married, where
I remember we were well entertained, and since I was with
governour Bubb and his lady with your son at Hampton.

Whether Kyrle arranged it or not, Elizabeth Budd accepted a proposal
of marriage from the Rev. Reginald Aubrey, sometime Vicar of Foy.
Kyrle, though having his responsibility halved by Elizabeth's timely
betrothal, doggedly pursued the balance of the debt, despatching
another letter to Madam Tooke.

Ross, this February 27th 1702.
Madam,-Meeting the bearer hereof, Mr. Philpot, in these
parts, I desir'd him to convey this to you, to let you know that
I acquainted Mrs. Aubrey, (Lt. Colonel) Bubb's eldest, with
your proposall, which wee consider'd, and find it so low that it
comes to little from money so lent from those persons who to my
knowledge at the same time wanted it themselves; and tis well

known that these children must have been in a bad condition had it not for myself. I know there was a great kindness between governour Bubb and your son, who entertained him and his lady at Hampton nobly. I was a witness to some of it, being with them two days. Whither he was able to do so or not, your son knew best, but it seems your nephew Bubb must pay for it. I have been told in what countrey your son is now in, and how he practises phisick there but I will not seek to get him arested, or to trouble myself with him, seeing I am to treat with your self a person of worth and goodness; therefore I beseech you to consider the low condition of your poor neeces and to send a favourable answer to, Madam, Yo' humble servant to com'and, John Kyrle.

Kyrle added:

Your neece Miss Jude presents her duty to you, who truly is a very good, and a fine girle, and a great scholler'. Addressed, -'to Madam Tooke, at or near Hampton, these present, Gloucestershire'.
(Seal, with a crest of a hedgehog or porcupine on a wreath.)

Irritated, Kyrle tried again, sternly reminding Buck that the matter had gone on too long.

Kyrle's pleading went unheeded. Further interest accrued. Buck never repaid the debt in full and nothing more was heard of him. Judith, a clever and diligent child remained with Kyrle as a 'general assistant', playing a significant role in his charitable projects, organising his affairs and signing and witnessing contracts, until 'her master's hand had become weak and tremulous'.

As for Colonel Bubb, he re-married, to a Miss Dodington, 'by whom he acquired a large estate, which came eventually, to his nephew, George Bubb Dodington, created Lord Melcomb in 1761'. In 1690 Bubb challenged two others for the position of Governor of Carlisle, a garrison town since the 13th century. After certain undemocratic procedures, Bubb won the seat by over a hundred votes thanks largely to the influence exercised by Sir Christopher Musgrave, for whom Bubb helped secure Carlisle during the Revolution. Bubb died in office two years later.

Abundance of Benefactors

Like many a market town in England at time, Ross had its share of rich men eager to set up charities to assuage guilt and ease their lonely journeys to Paradise. Others did so for less selfish reasons. Thomas Webbe of Monkton in Llanwarne, a carpenter who died in 1612, left enormous sums to the poor, including 'the sum of one hundred pounds for building a hospital in Ross for seven poor parishioners, and an incredible 'seven hundred pounds for the endorsement thereof'. Webbe also bequeathed £200 to render Wilton bridge toll free, adding 'if any of the said twoe hundred poundse shall remayne then the same shall be ymployed and bestowed by my executors towardes the finishing of the saied bridge or mending or makng the causey'. The indefatigable Webbe also left enough money to replace the rickety old Booth Hall in the Market Place. No one knows what became of Webbe's final donation. It certainly wasn't spent on building projects. The Rudhalls and the Westfalings, whose splendid tombs lord it over all in St. Mary's Church, were acknowledged as regular benefactors before Kyrle. John Rudhall, M.P. for the county in the first parliament of Charles I, succeeded to the family estates in 1609 owing to the deaths of two elder brothers. John Rudhall was serving as High Sheriff in 1636 when he died suddenly of gaol fever contacted at the Spring Assizes. A note in the register of Brampton Abbotts' Church confirmed that Rudhall and his family were so revered by the clergy that they were granted a licence 'for eating some flesh upon fishe days and in Lent'.

In 1653, Samuel Killing and his wife Elizabeth, who owned two houses in the High Street, gave ten shillings a year 'unto the poor of the parish'. The Markye family, whose name is associated with the Chapel in St. Mary's Church, founded an almshouse in Edde Cross Street for six poor parishioners. Charles Perrock made an annual payment of 30 shillings to be used as lamp-money for the altar. This figure was bolstered by an annuity of 26 shillings rent from property Perrock owned near the Market Place. In 1675, Perrocke (sic) gave 20 shillings to John Kyrle, and promised the same annually, towards 'Annuities to Rosse poore'.

The less well off were no less generous. In 1634, Richard Ballard, who lived in the notorious Helle in Ross, gave to the poor of the town every Good Friday, and in perpetuity, the sum of ten shillings. William Cator, who resided in the Pudding Croft, and John Cowles who lived near the churchyard, both gave ten shillings on Good Friday, forever. In 1654 Alice Spencer, as well as the bread she donated, gave what she could barely afford towards the upkeep of the almshouses in 1667, and decreed in 1677 that 'the poor in Rudhall's almshouses should also have bread every Christmas, forever.

A phalanx of relatively unknown benefactors were queuing up to hand out bread to the Ross poor. William Merrick, a mercer who lived in a tenement in Ross, in his will of 1641 left 40 pence to be spent on bread for 40 poor people. It was to be handed out by the vicar, in penny loaves, annually, in Broad Street, on Mid-Lent Sunday, after Evening prayer. The recipients were handpicked by the Vicar and the Churchwardens.

In the late seventeenth century, John Kyrle made a deal with Lord Weymouth to keep some of the tolls on the grain that was sold in the Ross market, providing flour to make bread for the destitute. On Saturdays, and in casual clothes, Kyrle smiled as he tossed small brown rolls slashed with the Holy Cross to the shawled and desperate who sprawled on the icy steps of the Market House. Bread was kneaded and baked by flour-dusted helpers in Kyrle's kitchen across the road. While observing the teeming throng, Kyrle was quick to drive away chancers from outside the borough. When the gift of grain was summarily cancelled, he was forced to abandon this sorely needed gift to the poor. The decision was not received with equanimity. Stratford refers to a letter, 'written in John Kyrle's well known bold and characteristic style of writing'.

> *Good Sir, I received your letter, wch I shew'd to Mr. Merrick, and wee returne you many thanks for your great care therin; tis a thousand pitties, but yt this thing should be well examin'd to ye bottom, therefore wee desire yt that meeting may be here which you have propos'd, and ye rather for ye rason you gave; and wee desire that you will be soe kind (as you have propos'd) to give notice to such persons as you see convenient to be here, and let us know your day, yt wee may be ready accordingly; and thus with my service to your Daughter, my little Goddaughter, whom I should be very glad to see, I rest yor kinsman and humble serv., John Kyrle, Ross, this 5th of December, 1695.*

The grain was not restored but the bread giving continued on. In 1706, Richard Knight, a Ross 'taylor', by his will, gave the rent of his messuage, burgage, or tenement in Brookend to the church wardens to pay for bread for the poor. In 1717, Christopher Mutlowe, of Brookend, donated monies to provided bread in perpetuity.

Tending the Sick

John Kyrle's charitable deeds progressed from handing out bread to tramping the unlit town, visiting the chronically ill and the mentally unstable in places where wretches coughed in corners and starving children piteously bawled. Helpless and friendless, the poor 'with sickness, want and a total incapacity to raise one penny, humbly secluded themselves in miserable courts and alleys, the healthy laying cheek by jowl with the gaunt and dying, with one chamber pot and a solitary bed per family.'

Kyrle, whose knowledge of medicine 'extended no further than kitchen physic', kept a closet by his door stocked with a few remedies made from plants and herbs. Trailed by a tentative young Judith Bubb, he pushed at unlocked and broken doors. With cures for cholera, anthrax, rabies, leprosy, tuberculosis, typhoid, diphtheria, tetanus and pneumonia yet to be discovered, ignorance and superstition abounded. Quacks sold dubious and often dangerous concoctions in Ross on Market days. Realising there was money to be made, dentists, surgeons, and, shamefully, even clergymen joined the quacks to sell 'cures' that sometimes had fatal consequences. Godfrey's Cordial, known to 'quieten babies with griping pains in the bowels', was opium charged and killed so many children it became known as 'Lord have mercy', alluding to the screams of hireling nurses upon finding their charges dead. Luckily for them they had Sibley's pill for the 'restoration of life in cases of death', which claimed to cure 'fits, strangulation, drowning', and improbably, 'assassination'.

Gentry too lived in fear of horrible diseases, using placebos from 'the closet of the eminently learned Sir Kenelm Digby Kt'. Digby's concoction was a harmless blend of white wine flavoured with rue, wormwood, celandine, sage, mugworth and mint'.

In common with many English market towns of the period, Ross did not have a dispensary with a nurse or apothecary in charge. A proposal to build a dispensary solely 'for the Nobility and the Gentry and other reputable persons and families', was unsurprisingly rejected. A free dispensary finally opened in Ross in 1825. Its first dispenser was Thomas Matthews, the chemist who purchased part of the Man of Ross's old house. By 1872 the Ross dispensary was treating 810 outpatients and moves were afoot to establish a cottage hospital. A letter of support was published in the Ross Gazette, challenging the working men of Ross to rouse themselves and support this noble work. It was signed Theophilus, a pen name for Thomas Blake, who offered a twenty pounds donation. William Hill, editor of the Ross Gazette supported the project by offering free advertising space. The embryonic hospital, comprising four rooms, opened in 1872, with Blake personally decorating the male ward. In 1886, the Man of Ross was remembered when a Kyrle Wing was built onto the back of the hospital at a cost of £120, paid for by the Kyrle Coffee House Committee.

Man of Property

Kyrle's name increasingly appeared on legal documents, alongside the likes of Viscount Weymouth, Sir Edward Harley, Sir William Merrick, William Markey, Francis Woodhouse and Margaret Scudamore. One profitable deal featured 'old lands, 3 acres, consisting of arable and coppice in Dymock, Rent 30 shillings at Annunciation and 2 pullets at the Nativity Term'. Kyrle would later own a wood in Dymock which had been enclosed in the sixteenth century. In 1665 it supplied cordwood to ironmaster Thomas Foley. Under Kyrle's ownership the Dymock wood yielded £100 a year in rent. After his death it descended to John Weale and others in 1727, and was still yielding a profit in 1763 when it was used to supply lathes, hurdles and hoops to ironworks in Powick, Lydney and Flatley.

A tripartite agreement Kyrle formed with John Smith of the Inner Temple and Roger Wintour of the New Inn, London, dealt in larger properties. In 1694 Kyrle was involved in the sale of a grand house described in the contract as a 'Capital messuage called Over Ross, and lands which include manorial rights'.

Kyrle represented Margaret Scudamore of Treworgan, Widow of Rowland Scudamore who was buying Tomlin Field, and all the land John Weare, yeoman, of Llantillio Crossenny, owned in St. Waynards for the hefty sum of £400.

Old Hill Court, in the scattered village of Hom Green, south of Ross, was in its time owned and inhabited by the Kyrles and the Clarkes,

Indenture dated 1708 (Hereford Record Office) ——

1708

This Indenture made [...] [...] by [...] Grace of God Queen of Great [...]
of [...] Burrough of Rosse in the County of Hertfour[d]
Elner Taylor of the other part Witnesseth
shillings and [...] cent of good and lawful money of [...]
[...] of the rents and covenants hereafter in and by these presents reserved and [...]
[...] to be paid and performed Hath demised granted and to farme letten [...]
[...]urell his heirs and Assignes All that parcell of ground known by the n[...]
[...] three acres of arrable land and one acre of Coppice wood ground
[...]ted of the said John Hyule and no others with all profits and emolum[...]
[...]th formerly enjoyed the same All which said lands are sett lying and b[...]
[...]th [...]morec Woods on the northside the land now or late of one Guy Win[...]
[...] unto the said Thomas [...]urell his heirs & Assignes from the day of the date here[...]
[...]uing & fully to be compleate & ended If he the said Thomas [...]urell Elisa[...]
[...] County of [...] or any of them shall so long live Yeild[...]
[...]heires & Assignes the yearly rent of Thirty shillings of good and lawfull mo[...]
[...]ule of good Pulletts att the feast of the Nativity of our blessed Saviour[...]
[...]etts to be behind & unpaid for the space of eight & twenty dayes next aft[...]
[...]and for the said John Hyule his heires & Assignes into the said demised [...]missed
[...]distreine and carry away & the same to keep & detain until the said yearly r[...]
[...] satisfied and paid unto the said John Hyule his heires & Assignes [...]
[...] with the said Thomas his heires & Assignes by these presents in ma[...]
[...] Authority to grant the premisses & every part & parcell thereof [...]
[...]urell his heires & Assignes paying the rents & performing the cov[...]
[...]foure & nineteen yeares if the said Thomas [...]urell Elisabeth [...]
[...] quiett possess & enjoy the said lands with their & every of their ap[...]
[...]d discharged or else well and sufficiently saved & kept harmless by [...]
[...]tts & rents paym[ents] incumbrances whatsoever heretofore had m[...]
[...] heires or Assignes or by any other person or persons whatsoever [...]
[...]urell doth for himselfe his heires and Assignes covenant [...]

two of the most eminent dynasties in Herefordshire between the sixteenth and nineteenth centuries. The new Hill Court, also known as The Hill, was constructed in 1698 for Richard Clarke who died in 1702. The Man of Ross was reputed to have been involved in both the design of the seven bay, two storey mansion, and the moulding of the agricultural surroundings into signature paths, patios and rose beds. The 'window' cut into a yew hedge to artfully frame the gaunt flanks of Goodrich Castle, is said to have been Kyrle's idea. He also may have planted the fine rows of elms that lined the avenue right to the imposing mansion house until they died and were replaced by oaks in the 1930's. The Man of Ross is credited with repairing and altering the churches at Foy and Much Marcle, and St. Mary's church 'shared in Kyrle's generosity too in a gallery and pulpit'. It is hard to find documentary proof of this, but the four-sided pulpit, with moulded and enriched cornice and panelled sides with bolection-moulding and inlay was installed in Kyrle's lifetime.

As Kyrle became more important in business, he used the suffix Gent, after his signature on important documents. He continued to help the poor facing eviction, despatching a note to the landowner asking for time to clear the debt, attaching a character reference of the distressed individual.

Isaac Tayor included on his 1754 county map of Herefordshire, Kyrle's Brook, a spidery squiggle leaking from sloping ground above a bend in the Wye. After rain this streamlet still meanders south, wriggling under the 'sixties built Ross to Monmouth road, snaking through a tangle of willow, blackberry, sloe and hop before tipping into the Wye at Weirend. Sadly, Kyrle's Brook has vanished from subsequent maps. Kyrle's Cross still exists, occupying a quiet corner near Peterstow Common. Kyrle Lodge, Kyrle House, Kyrle Gables, and Kyrle Meadow on doors and front gates, confirm the connection with the Man of Ross. Taylor, who was baptised at St.Nicholas, Hereford on October 4th, 1720, four years before Kyrle died, had by 1780 become an estate agent and timber merchant, operating out

Sketch of Kyrle's Summer House
Sketch of Vandervort Kyrle's Summer House, by Miss Riley

of Wilton and Peterstow. He died in 1788 and was buried in Ross graveyard. His grave remains unmarked to this day: another eminent person disowned and forgotten.

Kyrle's property interests continued to expand. On March 20th, 1707 he was involved in an Indenture tripartite between Richard Snead and his wife Mildred, John Smith of the Middle Temple, and Roger Wintour of the New Inn London. This involved land within the Manor of Broxwood, called Woodlands Fields, Henleys Field Hobbins Meadow, Killen Fields and Sillers at a modest rent of £6. On February 2nd, 1709, he signed a contract to lease to Thomas Murrel, a tailor of Dymock, Limetree leasow and the old lands (three acres) consisting of arable and coppice, with Dymock's Wood on the south side. The term was 91 years or the lives of Elizabeth Murrel (sister) and Thomas, son of Joseph Billingham of Newent, flax dresser. Witnesses were the ever-present Judith Bubb, and the Rev. Thomas Rosse, Thomas Webb and Thomas Smyth. On April 20th, 1711, Kyrle sold a small meadow to John Merrick, innkeeper, of Ross and was still doing business with Merrick on April 1st, 1721. On May 4th, 1713, Kyrle and James Collins, of Ross, leased five tenements in Ledbury; a messuage called the Crow at Upton Bishop, and a parcel of land in Upton Bishop, from William Collins senior of Upton Bishop and Mary, his wife.

Summer Houses

Kyrle owned a number of 'summer houses'. Called 'a pretty thing in its time', by Stratford, one ended up in Mr. Powle's half of Kyrle's garden when his house was divided. Thomas Matthews, the dispensing chemist, who owned the other half of Kyrle's house, also had a summer house. Erroneously described as 'Kyrle's summer house', it is a 'solid sandstone, Gothicke building with quaint carvings, narrow windows glazed with coloured glass, grey stone finials and gables surmounted

Bryant's 1835 map showing Kyrle's Walk (Hurley Collection) ——

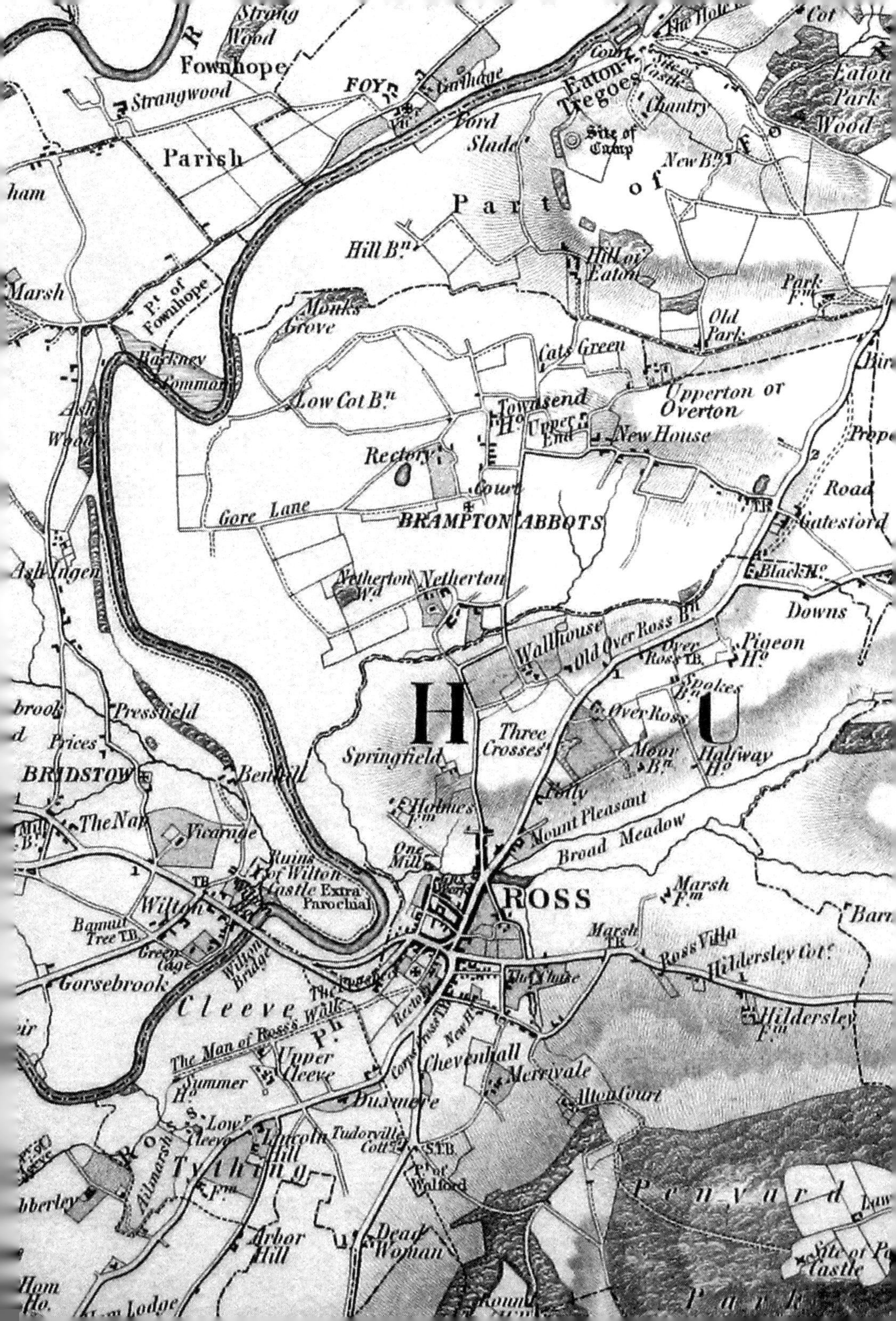
Strong Wood
Fownhope
Strangwood
Parish
FOY
Carthage
Eaton Tregoes
Site of Castle
Chantry
Eaton Park Wood
Ford
Slade
Site of Camp
New Bn
Part of
Hill Bn
Hill of Eaton
Park Fm
Old Park
Marsh
Pt of Fownhope
Monks Grove
Hackney Common
Cats Green
Low Cot Bn
Townsend
Upperton or Overton
Upper End
New House
Rectory
Court
Road
Gore Lane
BRAMPTON ABBOTS
Gatesford
Ash Ingen
Netherton Wd
Netherton
Black Ho
Downs
Wallhouse
Old Over Ross Bn
Over Ross T.B.
Pigeon Ho
Spokes Bn
Pressfield
Prices
Over Ross
H
Three Crosses
Springfield
Moor Bn
Halfway Ho
BRIDSTOW
Benhill
Folly
Holmes Fm
Mount Pleasant
The Nap
Vicarage
Broad Meadow
Ruins of Wilton Castle Extra Parochial
One Mill
ROSS
Marsh Fm
Wilton
Bamut Tree T.B.
Green Cage
Wilton Bridge
Marsh T.B.
Ross Villa
Hildersley Cotg
Gorsebrook
Cleeve
The Man of Ross's Walk
Hildersley Fm
Upper Cleeve
Chevenhall
Merrivale
Summer Ho
Bunmere
Alton Court
Low Cleeve
Lincoln Hill
Tudorville Cottg
S.T.B.
Tythin
Pt of Walford
Penyard
Arbor Hill
Dead Woman
Site of Penyard Castle
Park
Hom Ho.

by crockets'. It once boasted 'a serpentine walk through unmortared boulders and a rustic bridge'. The porch has a floor made with horse's teeth depicting a swan. Prince George of Cambridge visited in 1835, and is commemorated by a tablet.

Kyrle's favourite summer house was by the Wye at the end of his famous walk. Described a century later, as, an 'agreeable retreat, with a pleasing view of the river', Heath promised the visitor 'would not regret his walk, in extent about a mile'. Kyrle regularly strolled to his summer house, after a day administering to his benevolent causes, his gardening and his various property interests. The building was a glorified gardening shed, a simple wooden structure situated on the left bank of the Wye. A sign said it was not open to public inspection, as it was about to collapse. Stratford described the building as modest, where 'the venerable Man of Ross often spent his afternoons or evenings in quiet contemplation'.

When Kyrle died, his cousin Vandevort, who inherited the Kyrle estate, re-built the summer house at the end of the John Kyrle walk out of money he made felling some of the Man of Ross's beloved trees. A summer house is depicted on Isaac Taylor's 1786 map of Hereford, and on Bryant's 1835 map, which also shows the walk arrowing from the southern Kyrle Gate leading into the Prospect, between an avenue of elms along the boundary of Upper Cleeve, to a clearly marked 'Summer Ho', a mile away. In reality the path twists, and closely hugs the escarpment above the river. Kyrle, even in his dotage, would not have taken more than half and hour to walk it, admiring as he did, Penyard and Chase Woods, and if stopping to catch his breath, turning to view the magnificent spire of St. Mary, towering above the tenements and inns that surrounded it. The fields were cereals, pasture and plough in Kyrle's time, with hardly a dwelling or barn in sight.

Winifred Leeds, a Ross historian, cranked up the excitement with a suggestion that 'the benevolent Man of Ross, would spend his evenings in his summer house with his friends', including the poet Alexander Pope, while guests 'gave to certain of Pope's admiral productions,

Littlewood, where the Man of Ross planted trees three centuries ago ——

their form and finish'. Proof of this potentially fascinating meeting is lacking, but a publication entitled *Residence and Garden of John Kyrle* mentions an engraving featuring Kyrle's Summer-house, 'nearly in the same state as it was left by himself and Pope'. It speculates on how Kyrle and 'the man of letters' become acquainted. It is an intriguing suggestion but a red herring, one of many associated with John Kyrle.

A field currently belonging to Stephen Hay of Lower Cleeve Farm, called 'summer house field', on the 1823 Field Names map, is still known by that name. Kyrle's walk, one of the oldest town walks in England, survives. Well maintained, it is enjoyed throughout the year by locals and visitors to this delightful and historic place.

Obsession with Elms

Driven by 'the extensive use in the iron mills' in the late sixteenth and seventeenth centuries, and an industrial demand for charcoal, rotational coppicing began to dominate woodlands. Kyrle's decision to plant a wood in Dymock was based on sound business principles. On hills above the Wye, and the soggy plains below, Kyrle and his team relentlessly planted trees in serried rows. It was said that without Kyrle's trees, Ross would be nothing so far as the picturesque was concerned. A chronicler in 1684, confirmed that Kyrle even 'adorned the churchyard, which was an acre in extent, enclosed within a brick wall. All four sides were planted'. A tribute to the longevity of the elm is paid by Martin Morris, former editor of the Ross Gazette and honorary Bailiff to the Lord of the Manor, Manley Power. King's anecdotes states, 'the planter's taste for prospects is commendable; and it is said that by a vast plantation of elms, which Kyrle disposed of in a fine manner, he made one of the most entertaining scenes the county of Herefordshire affords'.

Morris reveals in the book on Ross on Wye, that many of the elms 'reputedly planted by Kyrle fell in the gales of January 1974. They were ravaged by Dutch elm disease. The rest were felled within a few weeks'.

Nell Gwynne's reputed birthplace in Hereford, shortly before its demolition - possibly in 1857 (Hereford Reference Library)

The elm was particularly adaptable for 'avenue planting' in towns, due to its calming beauty and the speedy rotting of its fallen leaves. Also, the tough, flexible wood was in demand for wagon wheel hubs, chairs and coffins. The elms were also planted as a wind break. Ancient survivors can still be spotted in English hedgerows. In the garrulous company of his labourers, Thomas Bevan, William Digwood, Thomas Jowling and 'Mad' John Rufford, the colourful cider quaffing quartet immortalised by Heath, Kyrle would have been content to plant elms all day. Being close to Kyrle, the labourers, particularly Rufford, became familiar. On one occasion, as the men, sweaty and dirty, paused for a cider break, the mouth of the communal jug was swiped with a dirty hand and passed around. When it halted at the boisterous Rufford, it could not be wrenched from his grip until he had swallowed the last drop. An exasperated Kyrle admonished him, saying, 'John, why did you not stop when I called to you?' Rufford leered, 'You can't 'ear nothin' when you're drinkin.'

Kyrle's expertise in tree growing did not escape the attention of the Crown authorities, who in 1692 engaged him as a Commissioner to inspect the trees in the Forest of Dean, and 'carry out its weighty instructions for investigating the condition of the same and reporting thereon'. Kyrle perambulated the Forest of Dean, studiously examining the condition of the trees. 'Practically acquainted with the duties entrusted to him and conscientious in the discharge of them', He was in his element, his new duties 'well accorded with his tastes'.

Kyrle's passion for tree planting carried on into old age, when he was content to work with pensioners like himself. Joseph Spence states that he employed 'very old men, such as whose infirmities rendered them incapable of doing such very hard labour, as the farmers required their servants to do'. Kyrle was happy to supervise these men and pay them amply for their labour. Some he sent into the woods and fields to pull up tiny, self-sown oaks, ash and elms, which were used 'to embellish the hedge-rows of his walks and estate'.

It was fitting, if fanciful, that when a dying elm root close to the church foundations threw out fresh tendrils, they insidiously entered the church and headed unerringly to Kyrle's pew. S.C. Hall, in *Pilgrimages to English Shines*, substantiated the miracle 'Beside (Kyrle's) pew, trees which have forced their way beneath the window in the wall, grew with great luxuriance, nearly covering the glass. They are slight and elegant elms, which when in full leaf are singular adornments of the sacred edifice as they wave their branches over his pew, and are regarded with much veneration'.

A half a century later, Stratford confirmed that the Kyrle elms were not merely visible in the 1890s, but, 'were great objects of attention, admiration and wonder'. It is alleged they were strapping specimens, as thick as a man's arm, 20 feet high. Due to hot house position by the window, the elms came to leaf early, 'the delicate green tints of the leaves contrasting with the barrenness outside'. They survived into the latter part of the nineteenth century, until they were fatally damaged when the church was refurbished. With regard to the 'miracle' of the elms uncannily knowing in which pew Kyrle prayed, it later transpired that Kyrle prayed in quite a different pew to the one embraced by the affectionate, if misguided, elms.

Special Friend

Kyrle's closest friend was the Reverend Charles Whiting, MA, DD, who became Rector of Ross on June 15th, 1699. Whiting was a man of genuine piety and Christian benevolence, 'who was greatly instrumental in forming the character of the Man of Ross'. He studied at Wadham College, where women were barred, with the exception of a laundress who had to be of 'such age, condition, and reputation as to be above suspicion'.

As their friendship grew, Kyrle and Whiting worked assiduously on a series of charitable ventures in Ross, including the setting up of a Grammar School in a corner of the parish church graveyard on the footprint of a crumbling messuage which was formerly 'among the ancient possessions of the chauntry priests in the church of

Ross'. Known as Saint Maries, or the Church House, it had an oratory and a private altar where clergy and other devout persons, 'were therein buried'.

'In chantry foundations of persons of rank and wealth, the endowment often provided for the establishment of an alms house, or hospital. Here were housed and maintained a number of poor men, Bedesmen, to whom the chantry priest, usually master of the hospital, served as chaplain as well as distributing Bedesmen's allowance, fuel and clothing, generally a long cloth gown of dark hue, bearing the cognizance of the founder on one sleeve. They were under obligation of attending church daily to pray for the late benefactor'. The men literally prayed for their suppers, and sometimes, depending on the generosity or not of the late benefactor, it was a long and unrewarding stint.

After the Dissolution there were certain claims made on the chantry building, including plans to turn it into a Grammar School. However, due to ownership and boundary queries, the rector claiming the rent it engendered, and churchwardens laying their claim due to their usage of it, and with the ancient lords of the manor of Ross Borough also expressing an interest, the building continued to decay.

Kyrle proposed to settle the question of right by first tackling the churchwardens' claim. As the latter could show no ancient possession, nor any title, his alleged usage was adjudged 'to have originated in error'. The rector too could produce no evidence to support his right to the building. However, his claim of renting the premises, though not regularly paying rent, was allowed. The result was that the Lord of the Manor of the borough, Thomas Lord Viscount Weymouth, in whom the estate was vested, was adjudged the rightful owner, with proof of several ancient presentments confirming his claim.

Through his agent, John Mainwaring, Gent., in 1704, Lord Weymouth 'gave and delivered to Charles Whiting DD, Rector of Ross, and to John Kyrle, Esq., the possession of the premises to the intent that the same should be and remain to the use of the said Dr. Whiting as the master of the grammar school there, and future masters of such school for ever, for the instruction and education of youth therein, according to the doctrines and usages of the church of England as established by law'.

Weymouth, by deed dated November 2nd, 1709, 'settled an annuity of £10 on a master who would be appointed by the owner of Ross Manor'. When at the end of the eighteenth century the Grammar School was succeeded by a National School, Weymouth's gift of £10 was passed to the Walter Scott School, 'to provide education and clothing for one extra boy beyond the number on the foundation'.

Whiting, was also involved in the setting up of the Bluecoat School in 1709, with fellow Oxbridge educated, Lord Viscount Scudamore, a noted agricultural improver, and other 'pious persons of the Nobility and the Clergy'. The Charity School accounts of 1709 confirm that John Kyrle was one of the 'pious persons' who assisted with its financing by donating £40 to trustees to purchase land, the rent of which was payable to the Charity School as long as it should continue, and then to Rudhall's almshouses in augmentation of their funds'. The Bluecoat school continued to receive the interest on Kyrle's donation. The sum was regularly collected by John Weale until he resigned at the end of 1743, at which point interest payments were suspended by the Trustees 'until a proper person could be found to lay out the said legacy, according to the Will of the Man of Ross'. Winifred Leeds says Kyrle's annual sum was subsequently lost, and blamed the carelessness of the Trustees.

The Blue Coat school was run on strict Church of England lines, with the boys and girls, sons and daughters of tradesmen, 'educated in the Christian Religion, according to the Doctrines and usages of the Church of England, as by law established, and for the clothing and otherwise assisting of such poor Boys and poor Girls, as far as the means of such School or Schools should extend for the doing of the same'. The school accommodated thirty children of each sex. Students were expected to be at their desks from early in the morning to late afternoon, with short breaks in between. Discipline was hard, with bullies and the inattentive having their trousers lowered in front of their peers, their arms and legs pinned, while their bottoms were thrashed with dry beech twigs.

Sunday mornings and afternoons the children, scrubbed and smartly turned out, marched to Ross Parish Church clutching their prayer books. The boys in their final year wore blue coats with red collars, blue waistcoats and leather breeches with lighter blue stockings, hats instead of caps and black ribbons around their necks. In case there was any doubt about who was paying the bulk of the money to finance the school, the scholars wore large tin badges upon their breasts, humiliatingly inscribed in black letters 'Walter Scott's Charity'.

John Kyrle was attracted to schools and enjoyed visiting teachers and pupils. He regularly attended the large, basic and overcrowded school adjoining the churchyard run by Verger William Dobb's very capable mother. Kyrle's unwarranted intrusions were for the bizarre purpose of inquiring which children deserved encouragement and which needed 'reproof'. Why the childless bachelor felt he had the right to instil discipline on others' children is hard to fathom. The students must have dreaded his visits, nervously twitching as Kyrle noisily clambered into a back seat, waiting for the opportunity to focus on someone whom he decided 'required censure'. Having chosen his victim, Kyrle pointed a finger at his prey and roared in a very rough voice, 'Ods Buds, Ods Buds, (God's blood!) I will mend you!'

The Rev. Charles Whiting died in 1711 and was buried in the chancel of Ross church. He was sadly missed, particularly by a grieving Kyrle who was godfather to his children. It was said that when school children were to be apprenticed, Kyrle 'was usually concerned', and sometimes 'put out other poor children at his own expense, to many of whom he was Godfather, - an office he seldom refused'. The Rev. Whiting, whose coat of arms contained a pun on his name, three whiting swimming, left a cheerful epitaph.

> *Here are deposited the remains of Charles Whiting D.D.,*
> *the unworthy (but most beloved) Rector of this Church, who*
> *died October 25th in the year of our salvation. Readers,*
> *thou art informed in these words, which (through his*

modesty) he would only have recorded, that he was a man of
ability, urbanity and learning; especially, that he was every
where famous for his excellent Preaching; and was Canon-
residentiary of the Church of Hereford.'

The Great Bell

In 1695, John Kyrle's Tenor, or Great Bell, was hung in the bell tower of St.Mary's. It weighed over twenty-four hundred-weight and was the second heaviest bell presented at the time. It was made at the Rudhall foundry in Gloucester. Kyrle was present at the casting, his ruddy face flushed by the roaring furnace. Then, with a celebratory swig of cider from a silver tankard, and a defiant roar, 'To Church and King', he flung tankard and cider into the bubbling crucible. With a diameter of 50 inches and a strike-note that is approximately D-natural, the Great Bell is inscribed 'John Kyrle of Ross, Esqr: Gave this bell: A.D: 1695'. The huge oak bell frame was installed in 1881 by Messrs. George Day and Sons, of Eye, Suffolk. It consists of heads, cross braces and sills, with strap-bolts in angles, and tie – bolts through the heads, braces and sills. It rests on a deal floor laid on deal joists supported by two sets of ancient beams. A balanced clapper was fitted in the late 1960s. The bell was re-cast by Rudhalls of Gloucester in 1770. It is still in use and is rung in combination with its seven smaller brethren. Kyrle's bell still tolls the hour and is occasionally rung at funerals.

Stratford recalled one dramatic incident concerning the John Kyrle bell: 'It was thought remarkable when the heavy bell, with a thunderous crash, fell from its wooden frame immediately after Kyrle's funeral'. Mourners must have looked at the ceiling with awe.

On the occasion of Kyrle's Bicentenary in 1925, the Parochial Church Council decided to associate the Man of Ross's name with a new clock in the church tower. The fact that new clock would strike the hours on Kyrle's tenor bell did no harm to fundraising efforts, resulting in the necessary 237 pounds 13 shillings and 9 pence being swiftly raised. As an afterthought it was decided to add the Westminster quarter chimes. The Ross Gazette of July 9th, 1925, reported 'As heard on the Ross bells, the chimes are a distinct acquisition, the beauty of their tone being freely commented upon'. The Gazette agreed they made 'a most suitable memorial of the Man of Ross'. It is reassuring to know that Kyrle's Great Tenor, lolling in its oak cradle, dusty, green and 300 years old, still booms the passing hours over the chimney pots of Ross.

Golden Period

The year 1700 was a significant one for Kyrle. He was in robust health, influential and comfortably off. At sixty-three years old he was full of energy and ideas. His impressive black gates , hung on the southern entrance to the Prospect, were described:

> *1700. Erected at the expense of John Kyrle, the Man of Ross:*
> *plain, square-headed doorway with the date 1700 on the lintel,*
> *flanked on the inner side by Corinthian pilasters supporting an*
> *entablature and pediment with cartouche and the arms of Kyrle*
> *on the inner side. On the outer side are the letters J K and C R*
> *interlaced on the tympanum.*

Now crumbling but noble, the Kyrle memorial gates were described by Nikolaus Pevsner in his 1963 book on Herefordshire as 'very dignified, like some college gate at Oxford, with its Corinthian pilasters, its pediment, and its cipher and date'.

Occasionally apt to do something mischievous, even childish, Kyrle doodled with 'a certified list' of various distances from the Prospect, all in yards. This bizarre and quite useless information was inscribed on a small, square brass plate, with the year, his crest, his name, and his family's motto, and was fixed to the wall on the north-west corner of the Prospect.

Anno Domini 1700
Once about this place, 10 feet from the wall is 372 yards
A statute, or post mile is 1760 yards
Five times about this place, is more than a mile by, 100 yards
From Ross Church to Weston Church is 4098 yards
Which make two miles and a quarter and 138 yards
Eleven time about this place, is short of Weston church 6 yards
From Ross Church to Brampton Church, by the One Mill, is 2,780 yards
Which make a mile and a half 140 yards
Eleven times about this place, is short of Brampton Church 176 yards

At the bottom of this plate, on the left side were the Kyrle's arms and in Latin 'Trahit sua quemq; voluptas', which one chronicler freely translated as 'everyone has his own hobbyhorse'.

An Unfortunate Gaffe

The diplomatic, and sensitive Kyrle was disturbed to receive a letter from George Scudamore, whose family owned the valuable Monmouth Forge on the river Monnow, from 1676 to 1736. Scudamore accused Kyrle of making scurrilous remarks about him. A thrusting entrepreneur, Scudamore had built his business over several years until it became a fire and brimstone belching monster, comprising furnaces, bake houses, boilers, troughs, sheds, smiths' and carpenters' shops, a clay house, sawpits, cellars, offices, rows of cottages for workers, and a mansion house. Kyrle despised confrontation, and after giving the matter some thought, it was with reluctance he seized his quill and composed a long and subservient apology.

It seemed that while dining with a so called friend, Kyrle, his tongue loosened by cider, casually remarked that certain hard nosed gentlemen who owned 'good estates', made it their business to be

richer and richer', instead of sprinkling a little of their largesse
among the poor. The non too subtle inference was that any man who
scalped hillsides, poisoned streams and reduced verdant valleys
to withered grass and blackened stumps, with towering, sulphur
belching chimneys that turned the sky a sickly yellow from morning
to night, choking houses and schools, should pay something in the
way of recompense.

Scudamore responded with eye popping outage. Hurt and startled,
Kyrle, while admitting that Scudamore's name might have cropped up
in the free-wheeling atmosphere of private gossiping, prevaricated. He
was, he said uncertain as to what was discussed 'and couldn't think
that this discourse applied to you, Sir. But take it that it was, I speak
no hurt, for I think I should do very ill to speak against one that did
not deserve it of me, especially against yourself, from whom I have
received kindnesses'. Stiffening a flaccid sinew, Kyrle continued:

If I should be so base as to raile at you, certainly I had been a
madman so to doe in presence of a person that I very well knew was
like to be neare related to you; so I am sure that if the report that
was given you was any more than was before mention'd, certainly
the 'little Spark on the top of the Hill' invented it himselfe, as by
report he is good at. Pray do not harbour anything against me on
this account, for my salvation there is nothing in it. Your Friend,
and humble Servant, John Kyrle. Ross this 7th of February 1705.

It wasn't long before Kyle regained his confidence and he was soon
playing one of his schoolboy tricks on a small theatrical group who
were visiting Ross. On the first night he attended at the theatre
door, nattily dressed. The doorkeeper 'judging by the appearance of
Mr. Kyrle, that he was a person of fortune demanded half a crown'.
Kyrle went home to change. Upon returning, wearing the 'cloathes he
usually wore in the fields' the doorman told him 'only sixpence for a
farmer'. As soon as Kyrle entered the theatre, 'the audience rose from

their seats, and made room for him, inviting him 'to take the place he best chose'. Thanking the company, Kyrle asked them to remain seated while he went to the back seats, quietly reflecting 'that he never made two shillings so soon in his life'.

Weeping at the Well

John Kyrle had reason to feel satisfied. He had achieved success from a trying beginning. He owned a fine house in the town, which over the years he had substantially enlarged. He had several servants, Roger Meredith, his trusted keeper, Elizabeth Williams, 'a servant maid', and Margaret Barrow, 'spinster', another servant maid - and Judith Bubb, his devoted assistant. Kyrle had peace of mind and kept close to the church, participating in their rituals. It was customary for the leaders of the town, churchwardens and civic dignitaries, to make an annual perambulation of the town's boundaries. Parishioners, some carrying picnic baskets, rambled through un-gated fields and ancient woods. At a slow, perspiring trudge they clambered up Penyard Hill to visit the Gospel Oak. The original tree was within Penyard Park, where a clergyman in vestments traditionally read the gospel of the day. The holy tree has long since rotted away, its former position forgotten, hence the moving of the meeting point to Flaxridge, near Penyard, a place by a shallow stream fed from a concealed spring. Long before Kyrle's time Catholic priests and their flocks made a similar pilgrimage, the priests slipping on his vestments to read a tract from the Holy Gospels before giving their blessing.

A sprightly 72 year old, the Man of Ross was present at the 'parochial perambulation' on the 31st of May, 1709. Kyrle kept pace with the Rev. Thomas Rosse, a Ross curate and loyal friend who had often witnessed the signing of Kyrle's property deals. Churchwardens and parishioners followed behind schoolboys from the Bluecoat School, who were delighted to be released from their studies. As the crowd gathered by the stream at Flaxridge, the furthest point of the walk, Kyrle moved closer to the Rev Rosse as the vicar unclasped the sacred book. As he read aloud almost the whole of the fourth chapter of the gospel of St. John, 'the scenery seemed to associate with the subject, our Lord and the woman of Samaria'. Heads bared in supplication, parishioners listened with rapt attention. As the reading proceeded Kyrle 'was observed raising his hat to his face to conceal his tears'.

After the reading, the Reverend Rosse closed his bible, a signal for picnic baskets to be unbuckled, sandwiches to be unwrapped, iced cakes to be handed round, and tea and cider poured. The happy crowd sat bare-legged on buttercupped banks to eat, drink and chat. Recovering his composure, the Man of Ross forsook the cider he was offered, and instead he dipped a wooden cup in the moss fringed pool and swallowed a cooling draught of the cold, pure water that eternally pulsed from the concealed spring. At this point, Mr. Maddocks, one of the churchwardens, 'expressed a fear that Mr. Kyrle might take cold. 'No', replied the good old man, 'what we have been listening to has made my heart warm!'

The Flaxridge spring still bubbles untainted, creeping towards an outlet to mingle with Castle Brook, the stream that once hurried to help turn the waterwheel for the paper mill at Bill Mills. It now takes a more sedate route before joining the slowly moving Wye.

Active to the End

Instead of sitting in his room with a rug across his knees pondering his end, the Man of Ross continued to potter with his labourers, 'pitching and repairing' roads, planting yet more young trees, unashamed to be out in the open air while his relatives and friends must have questioned his sanity. Though well into his eighties, Kyrle continued to play his part in the everyday minutiae of the small town lawyer, receiving letters, and firing off replies. He instigated proceedings against Walter Roberts, on June 27th, 1721, to whom he sternly wrote 'Pray cause an appearance to be entered for me in His Majesties' High Court of

Chancery at the suit of Duncomb Pyrke and others, for which this will be your suffience warrant, as witness my hand, John Kyrle'.

Kyrle also had kept a proprietorial eye on the Rev. Aubrey, the man who married Judith Bubb's sister Elizabeth, offering to make some sense of the Foy vicar's bookkeeping. In a letter dated, October 11th, 1721, Kyrle wrote that 'I hereby own and acknowledge that the day and year before mention'd, the Rev. Mr. Reginald Aubrey, Vicar of Foy in the County of Hereford, stated his accounts with me, and I doe hereby give a General Discharge to the said Reginald Aubrey of all Debts, Dues, or demands whatsoever, in Wittness whereof I have hereunto sett my Hand the Day and Year above written'. Witnessed by Judith Bubb and Thomas Woore'.

Into nodding old age, Kyrle was constantly reminded of the King he loved, whose initials were almost within touching distance of the tip of his walking stick. Over his long life he had seen other kings come and go. Erskine-Hill wrote 'The change from Charles to James, and James to William, seems to have made little difference to Kyrle's sentiments, and the succession of different sovereign's names at the heads of the deeds he signed, continued through his long life, with no hint of dissatisfaction on his part. Such, perhaps, was one of the blessings of a retired and unambiguous life'.

The Man of Ross Dies

The life force that drove Kyrle began to fade. Growing listless by the hour he took to his bed and lay there for a fortnight with the everyday hustle and bustle of the market place, with hucksters haggling, dogs barking, cocks crowing in his ears. On November 7th, 1724 The Man of Ross peacefully drifted away after his first and last illness. His had been a long, healthy and useful life, easily surpassing man's expected span. Nineteenth century Register's Returns for the district proves that longevity was not unusual in Ross, with a number of residents, mainly women, living well into their eighties and late nineties, and some achieving the century. The average ages of six people who died in the Ross workhouse in 1879, was eighty-three years old, with three women attaining 83, 86 and 93 years of age. It was reported in the Birmingham Gazette, of May 23rd, 1796 that 'lately in Webbes's Hospital, Ross, Betty Virgo died aged 96'.

Stratford reported that 'some years ago, a septuagenarian, in gratitude for the benefit he had derived from the air and the excellent cuisine of the Royal Hotel, insisted on having painted in large letters on one of its outside walls 'Ici on Rajeunit' - here one grows young again'. Anne Evans was living proof of that. Two days before her death Evans 'was so well as to keep market with a piece of cloth she had made, and retained her faculties till within a few hours of her decease'. She died on October 21st, 1819, and was buried near the north-west corner of the church. She had lived an astonishing 110 years.

With Kyrle, death 'was a natural extinguishing, a gradual decay'. In the town, shop blinds were pulled, the superstitious covered mirrors, ewers, and bowls of water to ward off evil spirits. Soon after the benefactor's death was made public, his corpse was prepared for his lying in state. Whispering visitors, some strangers from afar, climbed the wooden stairs and shuffled to the parlour where the Man of Ross lay, his strong hands clasped. For nine days he lay there. Hung in black drapes, and lit with wax candles, the room was stuffy, the atmosphere sepulchral. At each end of the unlidded coffin, a black clad mute stood stiff as marble. No one was allowed to approach the dead man or to lift the pall. Hand bells were rung. It was a fashion at the time that when an old person died a bell pealed for every year of their lives. Mourners shuffled past or clustered whispering.

As a man of rank, Kyrle's corpse may have been bound in a woollen winding sheet, cut from one piece of material, with a hood and knotted at head and foot. King Charles II decreed in the 1600s that winding sheets were to be made of wool to protect the wool trade. Watched by a shivering crowd Kyrle's coffin was solemnly carried on the broad shoulders of his workmates, down the stairs and out into the street, passing the Market Hall for the last time, for the short and measured journey to his beloved St.Mary's church.

'...with dirges due in sad array
Slow thro' the church-way path we see him borne.'
Thomas Gray, (1716-1771)

'People came from all parts, far and near, some travelling up to twenty miles or more, walking or mounted to pay their respects and view the Man of Ross. But also to enjoy proceedings, never having heard or seen such a ceremony before in their lives'. Public respect continued to the very last moment. The church and the chancel were filled with spectators to hear the Rev. Dr. Robert Morgan, DD, Rector of Ross, read the service over the dead man's coffin. Dr. Morgan said Kyrle was 'sober and discreet, reverenced and respected by all people, and died full of years and honour'. The congregation murmured its assent, lamenting 'in a general strain of sorrow, that they would never again see so good a man'.

Parishioners edged nearer as Kyrle, their friend and protector, was about to be interred, not in a freshly dug grave beside his Prospect, alongside the mouldering tombs of his friends and fellow citizens, who regardless of their religious beliefs were made welcome at his door.

History relates that the Man of Ross was buried in a hole dug under stone flags in the chancel floor, at the skeletal feet of his great friend, the Rev. Charles Whiting D.D, whose wife lay nearby. The Rev. Prebendary Money-Kyrle thought it 'curious' that John Kyrle's burial place occupied a similar position in Ross church to Shakespeare's in Stratford-on-Avon. Why was Kyrle buried at Whiting's feet? It seems an odd request. It was also one Kyrle never made. In his will he clearly states 'my body I commend to the earth from whence it was taken, to be interred in Ross Chancel, and in such decent and Christian-like manner as to my executors hereinafter named shall seem most meet and convenient'. There was mention of his friend Whiting. The principal executors, William Jones and Walter Roberts, both Ross attorneys, made the decision. Kyrle's was a humble burial. No muscular mason waited with raised hammer and chisel poised to commemorate his achievements, or indeed even his passing. Ross's most eminent citizen was quickly buried under soft damp clay, and the stone flags replaced. The reason given for such haste was 'to avoid inconveniencing the normal running of the church'.

Compare the Man of Ross's hurried despatch with the elegant internment of his Marcle kinsman, Sir John Kyrle, who stage managed every aspect of his going, from painstakingly designing his own opulent mausoleum, in white and black marble, to actually supervising its erection. He even built the chapel on the north side of the church to house it.

Sir John Kyrle, son of John Kyrle's great-great-uncle Thomas Kyrle, of Homme House, Much Marcle, was enobled by Charles I in 1667 and was twice High Sheriff of Herefordshire. He rebuilt Homme House in the early seventeenth century after a disastrous fire, an event remembered in a cartouche above the front door bearing the date 1623 (and in the marital coat of arms of his parents). The estate boasts one of the finest summer houses in the West Midlands. Proudly standing at the summit of a large walled garden, the handsome, recently restored Gothick edifice is Grade I listed and well worth a visit.

Sir John married well, his wife having inherited Whartons, 'a stone building of pure Jacobean architecture'. Col. Robert Kyrle, 'the stony hearted, twice married rebel' of Cromwell's day, sold it in about 1650 to John Jay. Robert Kyrle, who left numerous bequests in his will, was buried in Walford graveyard, next to his last wife. The man of Ross was a trustee, with Sir Edward Harley of Brampton Bryan and Thomas Harley of Downton Hall, Hereford.

Sir John Kyrle invested in iron-making, leasing a mill and forge at Goodrich from the Earl of Kent. It was the responsibility of the lessee to maintain all aspects of the forge and mill while in his charge. The arrangement ended on a sour note when the Earl's steward, upon visiting the site, discovered that chimneys were in a poor and dangerous state and one large wheel known as the 'chaffery wheele' was out of true. Sir John also bought and sold property, purchasing, with Tobias Payne, the delightful Elizabethan mansion, Fawley Court, which was later sold to Lt. Col. James Money-Kyrle, of Much Marcle. In 1652, Sir John was described as one of the chief proprietors of Fownhope, a desirable village some four miles away. The modern visitor grips the iron bars that surround the tomb and gazes at the 'rank and fortune mausoleum' and the effigies of Sir John Kyrle and Lady Sybil polished by the hands of many an inquisitive visitor. Sir John's memorial is a jarring display of pomp, and at odds with the humble stones commemorating others long and quietly dead. The 'man of unaffected piety, jocose without venom, who retained his mildness of temper under the infirmities of old age' would not have minded one way or the other.

The 'News Letter', of November 19th, 1724, announced 'On the 7th inst. dyed John Kyrle, Esq., in the 88th year of his age, called by way of Excellency 'The Man of Ross, being famous in all parts of his work in and about that town'. Kyrle was described, 'as of an active mind, plain in his manners, easy of access, possessed unbounded goodness of heart, and was in all respects a very public spirited character. He was for many years, a blessing to the town of Ross and its neighbourhood, an assister of young tradesmen on their first commencing business, an assiduous healer of discord and contention, a friend to the fatherless and widows and died at the age of eighty-eight, with that calm confidence and serene hope such a life insures - a death which we all wish for, but few have the right to expect'.

William Dobbs, many years sexton of Ross, and by 1798 one of the few inhabitants with any recollection 'of the person and manners of John Kyrle, Esq', died in that year. Dobbs 'retained his faculties to the last moment of his existence; and retired to that asylum, which as verger he had prepared for thousands, with the utmost composure of mind'. Unlike Kyrle, Dobbs, when his turn came to depart, had an altogether livelier send off. Singers and ringers of the societies of which he had been a member, attended his corpse to the grave; and after internment, they assembled in the belfry, where a great deal of Herefordshire sorrow was shed. The singing, ringing and drinking commenced at eleven o'clock in the morning and the bells tolled three in the morning before the tears of the tankard had ceased to flow'.

Charles Heath wrote 'Mr. Delahay, the present Clerk, says, that his predecessor Mr. Hardwick informed him (and no person's testimony would be received with greater respect, not only from filling a responsible situation in the town himself, but because his father was a native of Ross, -resided in it all his life, -knew Mr. Kyrle perfectly well, -and had related to his son many anecdotes respecting him, -that the only monumental record to Mr. Kyrle's memory was a flat stone with the initials of his name'. Pope would later assert that Kyrle may have wanted to die in anonymity 'a deliberate act of self-effacement', though it hard to square that with Kyrle's eagerness to promote his name on sundials, plaques and by holes punched in doors. We will probably never know the efficacy of this aside. Amateur historian, John Roberts (1709-1776), who after assembling 'much valuable information about Kyrle', carelessly lost potentially priceless material.

Kyrle looked upon his trees as a gift to the people of Ross. In his will, he stated that, 'I have improved my estate by planting fruit and other trees, which are as well ornaments, beneficial to the same, I do hereby order, direct and desire, that no wilful waste or destruction shall be committed thereon, by defacing or cutting down timber trees before they come to their perfection, the same having been planted by my great care and industry, for the improvement of the said premises'.

Soon after the Kyrle's passing, men came with weapons honed to destroy swathes of his legacy. The elms he planted 'in Copse Cross field, above the turnpike, were felled, 'the axe visiting them with premeditated violence, their honours laid in the dust'. Whatever the justification, the swish of the axe and the groans of Kyrle's trees hitting the ground was heard all over Ross. To some, the Man of Ross left a legacy that gradually became a nuisance. His friends blamed 'clerical vandals', men of God who had turned away from the Man of Ross. The destruction of Kyrle's trees left a bitter taste, even though many of them had lost limbs 'thro being visited by tempest'. Others were in such bad condition that, had they fallen, they would have taken 'houses to which they adjoined' with them.

Ross seemed to be managing quite well without Kyrle's fatherly involvement. Maybe some had tired of the stoical bachelor's constant interfering with every aspect of their lives. There were other benefactors who gave anonymously, and died quietly like fallen birds, their dignity intact. One such was Richard Worcester, who in his will of 1511 left a small house in Hatter's lane, later Old Gloucester Road, which he endowed as a hospital. The Rudhalls and the Westfalings, wealthy families connected through marriage, were consistently prominent. In 1575 William Rudhall, donated large sums towards the building of sandstone almshouses in Church Street, on the site of an ancient hospice'.

Tampered Will

John Kyrle's will, signed and witnessed, was published on November 27th, 1722.

> *In the name of God, Amen. John Kyrle of Ross, in the Co. Heref., Esq., being very ancient but of sound disposing mind, memory and understanding (thanks be to God for the same) considering the incident infirmities of old age and the uncertainty, and being willing and desirous to settle things in order, do make and ordain this to be my last will and testament in manner and form following, that is to say:*
>
> *First and principally I recommend my soul into the hands of God that gave it to me, hoping and assuredly believing that by the meritorious death, passion and resurrection of my blessed Lord and Saviour Jesus Christ, I shall receive free and absolute remission, and forgiveness for all my sins, and be made a partaker of those*

heavenly mansions which he has prepared for his elect before the beginning of the world. And my body I recommend to the earth from whence it was taken, to be interred in Ross Chancel, and in such decent and Christian-like manner as to my executors hereinafter named shall seem most meet and convenient.

Kyrle then dispensed with all is earthly goods, leaving everything to his 'esteemed and well-beloved kinsman, Vandervort Kyrle, gent, son of Thomas Kyrle, late of the kingdom of Ireland, gent.'

Kyrle signed away a considerable fortune in 'freehold messuages (dwelling-houses with outbuilding and land assigned to their use), lands, tenements (a room or set of rooms without a house, alternatively, a piece of land held by an owner), any estate of inheritance, lying in Ross, also in Bridstow, Walford and elsewhere in the county of Herefordshire, and in Dymock, and Berkeley, or elsewhere in Gloucestershire, and rents and services thereof, for the use and behoof of the said Vandervort Kyrle, and after his decease, for the use and behoof (benefit or advantage), of Robert Kyrle, being the first male heir. Kyrle also bequeathed to Vandervort Kyrle 'all my goods, and chattels and personal estate of what nature or kind soever, and in whose custody, power or possession soever'.

Kyrle intended 'to preserve the unity of possession and enjoyment' of all his estates, 'as well free as copyhold, to the intent that the same be preserved in my name and blood as long as it should please God to continue it. And in regard thereto, I have improved my estates by planting fruit and other trees, which are as well ornamented as beneficial to the same, I do hereby order, direct and desire that no wilful waste shall be committed thereon by defacing or cutting down timber trees, before they come to their perfection or otherwise; the same having been planted by my great care and industry, for the improvement of the sd. Premises.'

Kyrle specifically desired that the coppice wood, called 'Dymokes Wood', should not be felled under sixteen years of growth, and that the trees left 'should not be fallen till the same shall respectively be full 32 years' growth or upwards'. His dying wish was ignored by Vandervort Kyrle, who sold the wood not long after Kyrle's death.

Kyrle left Judith Bubb £10 'to buy her mourning'. He had already 'made an (sic) competent provision' for her by putting her life in a valuable copyhold estate, held under my Lord Berkeley, in the county of Gloucester; but I do remit, release and discharge her from all demands, I now have, or hereafter may have against her upon any account whatever'. So Judith was handsomely recompensed for the years of selfless devotion she showed to her cousin and guardian, John Kyrle, who always treated his loyal 'assistant' with affection and respect. But one cannot help wondering what the unwed, and childless, Judith thought, her youth gone, and her hair silvering, as she stood at the ancient bachelor's graveside.

Kyrle also bequeathed £40 towards the purchase of lands of inheritance of the yearly value of 40 shillings towards the maintenance of the Charity School as long as the same may continue; and if the school should cease, he decreed that the rents and profits of the said lands should revert to Rudhall's Hospital in the church lane. He left £10 to Roger Meredith, his servant man, £20 to Elizabeth Williams, his servant maid, £10 to Margaret Barrow, spinster, another servant maid. Finally to his 'old workmen or day labourers', Thomas Beaven, Wm. Digwood, John Rufford, and Thomas Jowling, Kyrle left them 40 shillings each. All were to be paid within three months of his death.

Kyrle's last Will and Testament was duly signed by him, and witnessed by Daniel Fisher, Richard Panter, (both Attorneys, residing in Ross), and William Dobles. As Kyrle died without issue, what remained of his estate passed to Vandervort Kyrle, and his male heirs. Vandervort, 'a short, bull necked man' was 'an extravagant young fellow, much in debt before his accession to the estate; and the same temper continuing after his coming into possession, soon reduced his income'. Vandervort Kyrle had two sons, Robert and Walter and a daughter Elizabeth. When he died in 1727 Vandervort's newly acquired fortune passed to his eldest son, Robert. He dying without issue, it went to Walter, the second son. He too died without issue. It seemed the gift was tainted. At this point, having run out of possible heirs, the wily Mrs. Clarke of the Hill, confessed to Charles Heath, that she had persuaded Robert Kyrle to cut off the intail of the Man of Ross's will, which forbade women from inheriting'. Mrs Clarke pointed out that a great part of the Man of Ross's estates were copyhold, and these he should have passed in Court, for the purpose of his Will, when he settled his intentions, according to the custom of the manor'.

Kyrle's estate, therefore, went to Elizabeth Kyrle, and 'her heirs, male or female'. When Heath again interviewed Mrs. Clarke, on Friday June 10th, 1796, she was in her 62nd year, and 'had drunk deep from the cup of affliction'. Questioned on how John Kyrle's 'want of judgement with respect to his Will, not having been executed in a proper form, thro' which his estate was conveyed to a different branch of the family', Mrs. Clarke answered that 'we are not all born to be rich'. Ironically, the eventual beneficiary was Ross attorney Philip Jones, a breed whom the very mention of was enough to make the Man of Ross apoplectic. Jones had married Elizabeth Kyrle. The estate was soon back on the market and advertised for sale in the Hereford Journal of the 4th of February 1779:

> *To be sold by private Contract, together or in parts, the very valuable Estate, formerly belonging to The Man of Ross'. The greatest part situate within a quarter of a mile from the said town, the rest at Munslow, near Ledbury, in the said county, also three substantial houses in the said town of Ross, one of which is the well accustomed Inn, called the King's Arms, which with said estates, houses, &c. are together of the yearly value of £477, and consists of several very compact farms; with a great deal of very rich meadow land close adjoining to the River Wye. The Great part is let to substantial and punctual tenants (who pay all taxes, land tax accepted, which is at the at the low rate of 8d in the pound) under lease for twenty-one years, eleven of*

Kyrle's house today, through an arch of the Market House ———

was banned from attending university, voting in an election, or holding public office. By the age of 12, Pope's formal education was over. According to his biographer Sir Leslie Stephen, as a young man Pope was harshly ridiculed, the attacks by jealous rivals personal and hurtful. This 'touchy, moody, intriguing little man', Stephen wrote 'constantly sought coffee to soothe his enduring headaches. He slept little and needed constant attention during the night'.

Absorbing enormous pain and distress from his complicated medical condition, Pope hungrily devoured classical literature, teaching himself Latin and Greek. When Voltaire met him he told Oliver Goldsmith (1730-1774), author of *She Stoops to Conquer* and the *Vicar of Wakefield*, that when he entered the room and 'perceived our poor melancholy English poet, naturally deformed, and wasted as he was with sickness and study, he could not help regarding him with the utmost compassion'. John Gay, saw Pope's impish, jolly side, referring to Pope, as 'sitting with nine beautiful maids dancing round him; crityicism stood at his right hand and Pastoral on his left, he was crowned with Lawrel and seemed ye Genius of ye Place'.

Publisher Jacob Tonson was tipped off by William Congreve about the rising star. Realising the work was 'extremely fine, Tonson sent a note to the seventeen year old Pope, requesting the honour of printing it'. Three years later a pastoral poem by Pope appeared in Tonson's sixth Miscellany. William Wycherley, who would later become a close friend of Pope's, joked that when Tonson played the role of gentleman-usher to the Muses, 'Jacobs's ladder will raise you to immortality'. The delicate, physically wasted, but phenomenally talented Pope had the break he craved.

This beautifully wrought work marked Pope as a passionately aware and precocious talent. His Essay on Criticism was published two years later to delirious acclaim. Subsequent literary successes, *The Rape of the Lock*, in 1712 and *The Dunciad* in 1728, confirmed Pope's astonishing and unprecedented rise from poverty, rejection and disadvantage to

Record of adoption of the Bubb sisters by Kyrle (Hereford Record Office)
Property lease with Kyrle's signature and seal

4° ffeb: 1694 in p̄s xx̄

Quo die comp Johannes Kirle pater et alt quandam
Mariam Bubb nup̄ uxorem Jeremiæ Bubb Ar̄ —
dum vixit gen de Hoy in Com et Diōc Hereford
defunct ab intestat quello p̄ eam condito aut Declarat
issto ob 14 dies et ultũ ille obiit ab hac luce migrass
seq fuisse et esse Gardiañ siū Curatorem ad lites
ltimo assignat Elizabethæ Bubb et Judithæ Bubb junior
fil̄ et ovidue defunct Quare petijt Lras Adcōis bonoruꝯ
siurium et Dređ [?] defunct duran minoritate minor
andrarũ sibi sub idowa Cautione p̄ eam interponend
demandari et comitti ac sub xx̄

Jurat fiat Adcō et p̄ntur /

Hum: ffisher Surr

one of the most critically celebrated, controversial, and wealthiest writers of his era. Pope enjoyed fame. He loved to be involved, being important, noticed and interviewed, and like many modern celebrities he felt diminished, miserable and filled with doubt and self loathing as soon as the interviewer drew the door behind him.

Pope was fawned upon by the lordly who invited him to visit their estates: his head was turned. Painstakingly he copied their sculpted topiaries, blossom spilling urns, vine wrapped temples, lofty, and owl haunted towers, rustic ruins and man-made lakes. Pope's garden comprised five acres which Horace Walpole said the poet 'twisted and twirled, rhymed and harmonised into three sweet little lawns, opening one into another, the whole surrounded by impenetrable woods'.

In his grotto Pope could sit in peace with his friends 'undisturbed by the distant din of the world'. The grotto, Sir Leslie Stephen remarked, 'was better fitted for frogs than for philosophers capable of rheumatic twinges'. Stephen added, 'Popes amusing himself with his grotto and his plantations, directing old John Searle, his gardener, and conversing with his friends, whom he compliments so gracefully, is, perhaps, the pleasantest in his history'. London being accessible by boat, Pope made the trip many times, 'so much so that his waterman was a regular member of his household'.

Through socialising with the gentry, the diminutive writer encountered the merciless and the avaricious, but also the charming and the good. Lord Bathurst (1684-1775) for example. A graduate of Trinity College, Oxford, and Member of Parliament for Cirencester in Gloucestershire in 1705, Bathurst held the seat until 1711 when he proceeded to the House of Lords. A man of 'uncommon vivacity and good humour', Bathurst became Pope's loyal and forgiving friend

After years of frolicking with his social superiors, slavishly copying their outlandish schemes, Pope began to question the fashionably banal in which he had become straitjacketed. Wearying of his garish villa in Twickenham, with its pan piping shepherds, spurting dolphins,

Nineteenth century sketch of the elm tree inside St Mary's Church ———

rainbow hued rose beds and emerald lawns smoothly unfurling to the Thames, Pope began to preach the necessity of allowing nature in all its childish innocence to shine, especially in garden design. In his 1713 *Catalogue of Greens*, the poet reiterated 'there is something in the amiable simplicity of unadorned nature, that spreads over the mind a more noble sort of tranquillity, and a loftier sensation of pleasure, than can be raised from the nicer scenes of art'. Pope began to sketch his epistle on the frailties of mankind. He would challenge those who spent their lives in cushioned idleness, wasting their time on pointless fripperies.

How Pope got wind of the obscure Kyrle, who practiced his basic landscaping in the rutted and boggy fields around Ross, is the subject of conjecture. One of several theories is that Pope derived his information about Kyrle through some of Swift's friends, perhaps from Swift himself, whose grandfather died vicar of Gutheridge (Goodrich) and was buried there. Or, maybe it was via Robert Harley, the Earl of Oxford, whose family lived in Hereford and who in the past may have had dealings with Kyrle.

William Henry Cooke wrote 'that Kyrle was personally known to Pope, or that the verses respecting him were composed during a visit to Herefordshire, though locally credited, are contradicted by existing proofs, nor is there any warrant for the assertion that Alexander Pope was at any period a visitor in this county'.

Stratford, in a *Memoir of John Kyrle*, explained that it had been 'religiously believed that Pope heard about Kyrle from a family he was visiting at Over-Ross. The house belonged to the Catholic Vaughans. While this suggestion cannot be validated, there could be an element of truth in it. When the Vaughans experienced financial difficulties in 1694 and 1703, resulting from the sale of their property, the stoutly Protestant Kyrle, who allowed no bigotry to interfere with business, 'stood in trust for several substantial sums owing to John and Mary Vaughan and their children'. Kyrle accomplished the deal satisfactorily, for by 1703, John Vaughan, 'late of Over Rosse', was ensconced in

The King's Head, a former coaching inn since at least the 17th century ——

'Hundsome', now called Huntsham, a place still inhabited by a scion of the original Vaughan family.

However, the theory with the most traction suggests that while staying with Bathurst at Oakley Park, Cirencester, Pope's attention was drawn to a brief item in the News Letter of November 1724, concerning the death, in the 88th year of his age, of a certain Man of Ross 'who was famous in all parts of his work in and about that town'. 'In consequence of this', Duncumb states, 'the poet was induced to institute enquiries respecting this excellent old person'. Pope was intrigued by the idea of weaving into his work, 'a simple, pious, and generous figure who lived modestly and who worked in the fields alongside his own men'.

Surely this mud spattered paragon, who at his own expense laid out paths for the poor to walk, and planted trees to provide ' shady rows', ' was a myth? Pope needed to find out, because if he existed, the Man of Ross was just the person he needed to counterbalance the pompous vacuity and greed of some of the wealthy, cocooned on their splendid but often vacuous estates.

Pope had contacts in Herefordshire. He was introduced to Viscountess Frances Scudamore (1685-1729) of Holm Lacey, by her cousin Robert Digby, son of the fifth Baron Digby, who met the diminutive author in 1717 when the two men formed a close bond. It seems almost inconceivable that Pope never met Kyrle then. The Man of Ross was hale and hearty and lived only a gentle pony and trap jaunt away. Especially, considering the gardens at Holm Lacey comprised majestic woods, avenues of trees, dense yew hedges, panoramic views, gravel paths, informal rose and flower beds, even a summer house, 'with a flamboyant cupola on which appears to be a mounted figure', and walks to the banks of the Wye, all classically Kyrle-ian.

It is documented that Pope didn't visit Holme Lacey till 1725, a year after Kyrle's death, to discuss and engage in 'improvements'. The widowed Frances Scudamore was intrigued by the idea of liberalising gardening, shrugging off stern formality and encouraging nature to play its part. Her early death in 1729 put an end to Pope's plans, a pity, because Frances Scudamore represented, according to David Whitehead, ' an ideal type of rural lady, embracing the pastoral idyll-the female prototype of John Kyrle, the man of Ross'.

In the early 1800s, according to Brayley and Britton in the *Beauties of England & Wales*, the Duke of Norfolk, 'the present possessors of this seat (Holm Lacey) permits the mansion to remain unaltered, as a perfect specimen of the style of building preferred by our immediate ancestors: we can still survey the apartments which Pope so frequently visited, and where he wrote his 'Man of Ross' in the same state as formerly'.

Resurrection

In 1731, Pope wrote to his publisher Jacob Tonson, who was 'handmaiden' to Pope, as well as to John Dryden and a host of the most important authors of the time. Conveniently, around 1720-22, Tonson had moved from London to the Hazle Estate on the outskirts of Ledbury. It was a fine property, pre-dating the Domesday Book and formerly part of the manor of Ledbury. The Walwyns, who owned it for nearly two centuries, leased it to the Eltons, one of whom, Anthony, married Alice Scudamore, daughter of John Scudamore of Kentchurch Court. Among the gentry it is indeed a very small world.

Tonson had slipped easily into tranquil rusticity and quickly scaled the social ladder, sending crates of his own cider to the Dukes of Grafton and Newcastle and having his newly burnished coat of arms printed on Isaac Taylor's first map of Herefordshire, with those of Lord Weymouth, the Westfalings and the Walwyns.

On November 14th, 1731, Tonson received a letter from Pope: 'Dear Sir, You live not far from Ross. I desire you to get exact information of the 'Man of Ross. What was his Xtian and surname? What year he dye'd, at wt age? and to transcribe his epitaph, if he has one, and any particulars you can procure about him. I intend to make him an example in a poem of mine'. Tonson replied the following June, feeding Pope scraps of myth, gossip and barely recalled facts about the Man of Ross and his benefactions. It was enough to seed Pope's imagination.

Having tracked down his man, Pope wrote again to Tonson on June 7th, 1732: 'I intended to write to you my thanks for your great diligence (or let me give it a higher title) zeal you have shewn in giving me so many particulars of the Man of Ross. They are more than sufficient for my honest purpose of setting up his fame as an example to greater and wealthier men how they ought to use their fortunes. You know few of these particulars can be made to shine in verse, but I have selected the most affecting, and added two or three which I learned from other hands. A small exaggeration you must allow me as a poet, yet I was determined the groundwork at least should be truth, which made me so scrupulous in my enquiries; and sure, considering that the world is bad enough to be always extenuating and lessening what virtue is amongst us, it is but reasonable to pay it sometimes a little over measure to balance that injustice, especially when it is done for example and to encourage others. If any man shall ever happen to endeavour to emulate the Man of Ross, 'twill no manner of harm if I make him think he was something more charitable and more beneficent than really he was, for so much more good it would put the imitator upon doing. And further, I am satisfyd in my conscience (from ye strokes in two or three accounts I have of his character) that it was in his will and in his heart to have done every good a poet can imagine. My motive in singling out this man was twofold; first to distinguish real and solid worth from showish or plausible expense, and virtue from vanity; and secondly, to humble ye pride of greater men by an opposition of one so obscure and so distant from all ye sphere of public glory'.

Pope was subsequently accused of inventing 'the ideal townsman or civic leader with a degree of pastoralism we are not to take at face value'. His making Kyrle 'better in reality than his meritorious actions' shocked the literary world on the publication of the *Moral Essays* in 1733. Pope was so unsure of his waning ability as a writer and philosopher, he published the work anonymously. However, when the other parts appeared in print in 1733 and 1734, and were hailed, Pope was ready to claim authorship.

The Essay of Man was described as 'Pope's most ambitious project', one that was widely translated and helped spread his reputation beyond the British Isles. It was described by one critic as 'passionately executed, with the passage on the Man of Ross, outstanding'. It 'carried Kyrle's name throughout the world. No other town in England had such a protector and benefactor'. Kyrle represented, 'a traditional world of equilibrium where decent values went hand in hand with a sensitive appreciation of the pastoral landscape and gardening, seemed an ideal subject'.

Pope sent an early draft of the poem to a friend, John Caryll, in 1733, commenting that 'it is not the worse poem I have written; it abounds in moral examples. God send it does any good, I really mean nothing else by writing at this time of my life'. Lady Anne Irwin was also sent a copy. Writing to her father, the third Earl of Carlisle, on January, 18th, 1733, she said: 'I enclose you Mr. Pope's new poem. The Man of Ross is his hero; the lines which describe him are the best, in my opinion, of any in the poem'.

Pope's genius transformed the rejected Man of Ross into a silver maned, purple robed, cloud reclining deity, straight off a Sistine Chapel ceiling. Kyrle, whose life in many respects 'was that of a yeoman, too humble for the great issues of national politics to touch him deeply', would have blushed at his sudden lionisation.

The Essay on Man was translated into French and caught the eye of Voltaire (1694-1778), an industrious communicator, who wrote over 2,000 works of philosophy, poetry, novels and plays. Voltaire had fled to England after being accused of insulting an upstart in the French nobility. A prominent advocate of free expression, and an indefatigable supporter of social reform, the Frenchman became one of Kyrle's most ardent admirers, and in 1751 he wrote a poem on Natural Law, which was unhappily described as a comparatively feeble application of Pope's and Kyrle's ideas and principles. In his *Histoire de Jenni*, published in 1775, Voltaire wrote, 'Lock, Newton,

Tillotson, Pen, Clarke, the gentleman called the Man of Ross, so many others in our Isle and outside our Isle, that I could site for you, were they not models of virtue?'

Poisoned Arrows

Pope's beatification of Kyrle was met with outrage and dismay. Immediately, the character assassination began. The raising aloft of Kyrle was questioned in several quarters, even by an admirer, Dr. Johnson 1709-1784, who wrote;

> *Into this poem some hints are historically thrown, and some known characters are introduced, with others of which it is difficult to say how far they are real or fictitious; but the praise of the Man of Ross deserves particular examination, who after a long and pompous enumeration of his public works and private charities is said to have diffused all these blessings from 500 pounds a year. Wonders are willingly told and willingly heard. The praise of a good man, being made more credible, may be more solid. Narrations of romantic and unpractical virtue will be read with wonder, but that which is unattainable is recommended in vain. That good may be endeavoured it must be shown to be possible. The Man of Ross merely collected money from wealthy friends then allowed them to choose projects that they approved of, instead of those that would benefit all the citizens of Ross. Kyrle gave away very little, if any, of his own money.*

The Reverend Thomas Brome B.A., who like Kyrle, was a Balliol man, wrote in 1733, 'Kyrle was not the founder of the church, nor did he erect the spire, nor build a hospital in Ross'. An anonymous Ross man, who spent his life in the town and who knew Kyrle's relatives, told Charles Heath that there was a general belief in the Kyrle family that Pope, being much indisposed, had come to Ross to recuperate, and that Kyrle not only sought him out, but 'paid the poet every degree of attention that hospitality or kindness could suggest, in return for which civilities the Muse of Twickenham afterwards honoured him with a never dying fame'.

The bile continued to flow. Matthew Gibson of Abbey Dore, who married Kyrle's niece, while discussing Kyrle's character with Thomas Hearne on October 18th, 1734, responded to Hearne's remark that Kyrle was, 'an extraordinary, charitable and generous man, who did much good', with a slanderous outburst. While barely conceding that Kyrle did a great deal of good, spluttering, 'all out of vanity, and ostentation, Kyrle being the vainest man living'. Gibson accused Kyrle of hating his relations, insisting he 'would never look upon them, or do anything for them, tho' many of them were very poor'. Hearne later dismissed Gibson as, 'a crazed man, and withall stingy, tho' he be rich, and hath no child by his wife'.

When asked, if there was a particular reason for the Man of Ross being selected for Pope's praise, Mrs. Clarke of the Hill, an in-law as well as a friend of Kyrle's, 'replied in the negative'. It seemed that even Kyrle's kin believed that when the ailing, guilt ridden Pope said he visited Ross, ' for the benefit of the air', Kyrle immediately sought him out, clamouring to touch the hem of a man whose philosophy and extravagant lifestyle were totally alien to the thrifty and taciturn Man of Ross, who was happy living quietly among his own people in the small close knit town above the river Wye.

Even William Dobbs, the ancient Ross verger, whose mother ran the Dames' School (an elementary school run by a woman, the usual fee being three or four pence per week), also took exception to Pope's poem. The idea of the saintly Kyrle sitting in the freezing Market Place, his hat dusted with snow, his fingers icicles in their woolly mittens, was, Dobbs suggested, a calumny. As for Kyrle trudging about the dank town at night visiting those in Rudhall's almshouses, Dobbs laughed. Kyrle, he said, ignored the almshouses, whose endowment was the responsibility of rival benefactors, whose beautiful and ostentatious monuments still rear above all others in Ross parish church.

As for wandering beggars loitering at Kyrle's door hoping for a bone to gnaw? They were wasting their time. Kyrle showed scant interest in beggars from outside Ross, however needy they might be. Kyrle, Dobbs insisted, only gave to hard working locals temporarily down on their luck. When asked if Kyrle showed any kindness to him personally, Dobbs replied, 'excepting the instance of a loose copper coin, to buy a cake, or fruit in season. Those who founded their claim on Kyrle's liberality', Dobbs said, 'were quite small'. As for the seemingly endless queue on the Market House steps, day and night waiting for a handout? 'Kyrle's generosity', Dobbs said, 'was confined to feastable times, such as Easter, Whitsuntide, Christmas, and other grand festivals which our church celebrates'. He conceded however, that if the very poor, 'solicited relief at Kyrle's door, he might give them food or a little money'. But, Dobbs said, Kyrle rarely allowed visitors in his house, 'and kept so few domestic servants, that the dispensations from his own table must have been limited'.

John Wesley, founder of Methodism, asked in an article in the London Chronicle on January 2nd, 1761, 'does not the keeper of Newgate prison deserve to be remembered as well the Man of Ross?' The Reverend Charles J. Robinson, who studiously annotated the social climbing and ambitious intermarrying of Herefordshire gentry in *A History of the Mansions and Manors of Hereford*, originally published 1872, glared through his cracked pince nez at what he perceived to be the upstart Kyrle's sudden fame, when he intoned. ' it is impossible to omit all mention of John Kyrle, although our notice must be curtailed by our belief that he has too often been made the subject of extravagant laudation. A country Squire who does his duty to his God and to his neighbour, displays some public spirit and a zealous attachment to the Church of his choice, is we hope, not a very rare character, even in these degenerate days, and it is certainly one for which a parallel might be found in the annals of almost every neighbourhood'. Robinson added that Kyrle's benevolence 'had the good fortune to attract the notice of a poet whose Court and City life had made him almost a stranger to the virtues of out-spoken honesty and unostentatious benevolence.'

More of Kyrle's beloved trees were hacked down for firewood and 'monsters in the shape of men' wantonly smashed his sundial and threw it into the garden beneath. It was honourable to the feelings of the Town Officers that they offered a large reward for the discovery of the offenders, but its authors escaped the punishment they so richly deserved. On May 15th, 1771, William Mynd of Ross offered a reward of two guineas 'to anyone who will discover the person or persons who destroyed the trees planted in the Kyrle Walk'. S.C. Hall in 1851 added 'all that could do honour to the memory of the man, and continue his benevolence, from generation to generation, has been removed by one innovator after another, and the people of Ross are either so stupid, or so timid as to submit to this encroachment on their rights'.

The backlash continued. A chronicler in the early 1800s wrote 'the Prospect ground is now merely a field, yet enough remains to show (Kyrle) intended it as a parterre; and the Walk has been deprived of many of the trees that formerly shaded it, together with the seats for the weary traveller's repose. Along the edges of the rock, which forms the foundation of this natural terrace, the Sand Martin digs his hollow nest'.

The crucifying of Kyrle continued into the twentieth century. In 1925, Edward Foord commented, 'Kyrle owes a good deal of his celebrity to some rather absurd lines by Pope - so absurd that one wonders if the poet were in his sober senses when he penned them. One hears rather too much of the Man of Ross at Ross. He seems, without hyperbole, to have been a hearty, jolly, rather bluff and noisy country gentleman of the type satirised by Macaulay, with many eccentricities, but actively and discriminately benevolent. His extortions were of benefit to the town, which repaid him by bestowing on his memory a somewhat exaggerated degree of respect. There is nothing of interest in the monument. Kyrle himself is buried beneath the pavement near it.'

Saesneg, cowering under a nom de plume, wondered in the Hereford Journal of April 9th, 1927 how Kyrle had managed to become 'the patron saint of the town'. What did he do, beyond 'planting a few trees and laying out a not-too-good footpath? Hardly reasons to bring him immortal fame. Kyrle did nothing to give him any claim to be placed on a higher pedestal than any of his fellowmen'.

In 1952, when the Department of the Environment was listing buildings of Special Architectural or Historic Interest in the Urban District of Ross-on-Wye, the compilers, while noting details from a bust of Kyrle directly above their heads managed to get wrong important details of the most eminent man in the history of the town.

H.L.V. Fletcher, commenting in 1968, thought Kyrle too good to be true; 'What made him give, give, give? Why did he hate to be alone? When I first learned of the Man of Ross, that phrase *he appeared always discomposed when 'twas time to part* stuck in my mind. Suddenly Kyrle seemed a lonely man, without wife, close companion or children, a Pickwick with something on his mind'.

The Kyrle plaque, that was ripped off the Prospect wall and sold for a paltry sum to a dealer in old metal, was returned to Ross Town council. It languished unseen before again disappearing, only to turn up once more in the Council Offices, where it was valued in 1984 by the late Lt. Colonel Matthews, a specialist in 'period furniture, arms and armour'. Matthews suggested a figure of £500, with the rider that his fairly high valuation referred only to the people of Ross.

Matthews described the plaque as 'old and difficult to value. I consider many people would give £150-£250 for it, yet is almost priceless to the people of Ross - and of course irreplaceable. And being so small it would be easily concealed. And it appears to be fixed to the wall by a few small screws, i.e. one good pull would remove it. I strongly recommend this plaque be made a lot more secure'. The plaque used to be kept in the Council Chambers in Ross and could be viewed by appointment. A recent enquiry revealed that it cannot be found - yet another insult to the battered Man of Ross.

Even Erskine–Hill, an admirer, concludes on a sombre note, suggesting that 'while Kyrle's was in many ways a remarkable life, there is nothing about it that would have seemed brilliant, dramatic or striking to a society which increasingly looked to the capital for the most compelling human achievements and events of the time. Kyrle's life was unashamedly provincial; he might have been a man of the City, but chose instead that the significance of his life should be in the country, in the market town where most of his small property lay'.

In 1861, Hall pleaded that the 'prophet yet find in his own country other honours than those which give his name to a wayside inn, a walk of which he would be ashamed, and a house defaced by an unseemly bust of plaster'.

A Monument at Last

It was Pope's contention that those with the most garish and grandiose monuments didn't toss and turn in their feather four posters, worrying about starvelings shivering in dark and draughty tenements.

> *I was not sorry (Kyrle) had no monument, and will put that circumstance into a note, perhaps into ye body of ye poem itself (unless you entreat the contrary in your own favour by your zeal to direct one. I would, however, in this case spare censure upon his heir (so well as he deserves it), because I dare say after seeing his picture everybody will turn that circumstance to his honour, and conclude the Man of Ross himself would not have any monument in memory of his own good name.*

Kyrle's grave would remain unmarked, except for the scrap of wood bearing his initials and placed at the scene shortly after his death. As time passed, with no prospect of a more permanent memorial, the Rev. Whiting's son, who was Kyrle's godson, wrote to the Rev. John Roberts, (1709-1776).

> *Dec. 16th, 1748; Dear Sir, I could not but observe with some concern that my old godfather-the man of Ross-lies undistinguished, although his name is perhaps the best recital of his excellent qualities; yet it might not be out of character for me if a few words*

were placed over him. His age or time of death I do not know, and I
assure you that gratitude is my only motive in this affair. I suppose
an epitaph might be cut upon a piece of forest stone, at no great
expense, at the foot of my father's grave, where I understand he
desired to be buried.

Walter Kyrle, Vandervort's son and beneficiary of Kyrle's amended Will, objected to Whiting's interference. But in 1749 he had second thoughts and paid for a memorial stone to be set into the sanctuary floor, covering the vault 'holding the mortal remains of the good Man of Ross'. Walter Kyrle's belated memorial is a heavy, quietly impressive slab of blue slatey stone. Sited close by the busy altar, thousands have unwittingly trodden on it over the years; preachers, penitents, pilgrims and choirboys have all shuffled and scuffled over it, and yet the memorial is in remarkable condition, with Kyrle's coat of arms as crisp and legible as the day they were carved. The memorial bears this discreet inscription:

John Kyrle, Esq., died November 7th, 1724, aged 88

Other names have since been added, including that of Walter Kyrle's father, Vandervort. The full list includes:

Vandervort Kyrle, Esq., died October 5th 1727, aged 55
Robert Kyrle, Esq., died March 13th 1736, aged 31
Mrs. Francis Kyrle, died February 9th 1744, aged 67
Mr. Walter Kyrle, died January 14th 1775, aged 70
Mrs. Elizabeth Weale, died March 23rd 1779, aged 75 years

Stirred by Pope's praise of Kyrle, Lady Betty Dupplin, a 'collateral descendant' of Kyrle, left a sum of money in her will to erect a monument. Writing to Col. James Money Kyrle, her executor, she was 'desirous that a monument be erected in memory of my late cousin John Kyrle, called the man of Ross. I desire the sum of £200 to be applied for that purpose, and the character of him by the late Mr. Pope, collected as my executors shall think proper from his writings, inscribed thereon by way of an epitaph to be wholly in the discretion of my said executors.'

Commenting on the belated memorial to Kyrle, Samuel Ireland stated 'the design was made by a Mr. Marsh of this town, who has introduced a bust of the good man that bears little resemblance to either of the portraits I met with in Ross, one of these is in the possession of Philip Jones Esq.; a gentleman, who by marriage with a descendant of John Kyrle, enjoys all his property, and by his urbanity renders himself a worthy representative of that exemplary character.'

The much derided monument, now two and a half centuries old, with its plump hedgehog, sculpted cornstalks, autumn fruits and vegetables is in excellent condition as it gamely clings to the north wall of St. Mary's chancel, bearing the simple dedication 'This monument was erected in memory of Mr. John Kyrle, commonly call'd The Man of Ross'. A polished brass plaque below it is inscribed 'In virtue of a bequest under the will of Constantia Viscountess Dupplin, great granddaughter to Sir John Kyrle, of Much Marcle, in the county, Bart., Lieut.-Col. James Money, of Much Marcle aforesaid, her executor and heir, erected this monument, in memory of her kinsman, John Kyrle. A.D. 1776'.

Stratford was unimpressed, suggesting that Marsh's monument 'made at his statuary in Bristol' lacked the antiquity and imposing beauty of the grander Rudhall relics. The medallion purports to be a portrait of John Kyrle; the oval bas-relief design in the centre, surmounted with the cornucopia, is symbolical of Charity supported by Benevolence. At the base are the crest and arms of Kyrle.'

Kyrle's House

Part of Kyrle's garden at the rear of the house was later made into a bowling green, destroying the Man of Ross's blooms and flowering shrubs in the process. Bowling had grown in popularity in the eighteenth and nineteenth centuries. One day a week, the manicured green 'was the resort of the principal gentlemen of the town and neighbourhood, attracting up to 30 persons of the first consequence, dressed in their scarlet gold laced waistcoats'. Belonging to the exclusive Ross Bowling club was 'a great mark of favour.'

Among the more eccentric gentlemen who frequently ambled there to engage in conversation, and even try their hand at bowling, was Bishop Egerton, 'the father of tourism', who lived nearby. An aged Ross native who remembered the fragrant, white wigged Egerton, commented 'however strange it may seem to us, no bad consequences were found to result from such an intercourse'. Kyrle took no interest in sport of any kind and had he lived, it is highly unlikely the bowling green would have existed. For a while it was an attraction. Well behaved local boys were permitted to sit quietly on the wall that surrounded the green to watch the bowling.

When interest in bowling declined the boys on the wall were replaced by abrasive 'menials of the Inn, with beer jugs in their hands'. This unsavoury element took to using Kyrle's former summer house as a drinking den. Little or no care was taken of Kyrle's former place of relaxation and it inevitably deteriorated until it was ruined, like most things associated with the Man of Ross.

A sketch of the Kyrle property, showing the view from Kyrle's front door, was published in an 1823 edition of the Monthly Magazine. It clearly shows how close Kyrle lived to the tenement, known as Under Helle, a dingy 'secret place'. The wretches who lived there in Kyrle's time called it Hell and meant it. The former National Provincial Bank, now NatWest, stands on its grave.

Kyrle's property was sold to J.S. Collins who closed the inn and divided the house. One part was occupied by the respected chemist, Mr. Matthews, who modernised his portion, a task which involved some demolition. The other, a nest of old beamed rooms, was inhabited by Richard Powle, a stationer, printer, and bookseller. On the front of Kyrle's house is a panel with ringletted Kyrle head in bas relief, with the legend, 'Died November 7 1722, and aged 88'. Kyrle died in 1724 aged 87. The guardians of Ross even got that wrong.

In an extract from the Herefordshire, Vol.11-East, 1932, Royal

Commission on Historical Monuments, England, John Kyrle's former home is dryly described:

> *Nos. 34-36, S of the Market Hall, formerly the house of John Kyrle, the Man of Ross, is of three stories with cellars. It was built late in the 16th or early in the 17th century and has a long projecting wing at the back. The N. front has exposed, and fairly close–set timber-framing except to the ground floor, which has modern shop-fronts, and the upper part of No. 36 which is cement-rendered. The second story projects on a moulded bressummer with carved brackets; there is an enriched moulded beam and similar carved brackets below the eaves, formerly supporting a series of gables or other superstructure, now removed. The back additions are partly of stone. Inside the building, the ground-floor of No. 35 has original moulded ceiling-beams and on the first floor is some exposed timber-framing. The back room on the first floor has three walls lined with original panelling. The back wing has a roof with double collar-beam trusses; on the first floor are two late 17th century doors, with the date 1689 and the arms of Kyrle in punctured decoration.*

It was recorded in 1861 that Kyrle's house had been divided: 'one portion in great measure rebuilt; the other not so materially changed. The room looks out upon his garden, which has been divided like the house, the other into a bowling green, the surrounding wall of both, however, sustain flourishing vine and pear trees'. A large part of the attractive old house where Kyrle lived for nearly seventy years, and died, happily survives as number 35 in the High Street, Ross. After serving as delightfully Dickensian editorial offices for the Ross Gazette for over a hundred years, it continues to prosper as bustling stationers in the caring hands of the Coleman family.

Coleridge Pays His Respects

Upon inheriting Kyrle's old house, Vandervort's son Walter Kyrle let the property to Joseph Prosser, who converted part of the property into an inn called The King's Arms - an appropriate name given Kyrle's Royalist instincts. When Prosser died, Walter married the dead man's widow and proved to be a popular landlord, embellishing the King's Arms growing reputation as the most popular inn in Ross. Cosy and friendly, it attracted some who wished to just sit where Kyrle sat and to raise a glass to his memory.

In spite of Kyrle's sombre funeral, unmarked grave, butchered elms, smashed sundial and fountain filled with unspeakable garbage, his legend prospered. In the late eighteenth century The King's Arms became an unlikely target for tourists who made the long journey to Ross to peer over the fence at Kyrle's modest garden, walk his walk and clamber over the gothic Summer House, which had nothing whatever to do with the Man of Ross.

One special pilgrim was Samuel Taylor Coleridge, (1772-1834) a manic depressive opium addict, and author of the blood curdling *Rime of the Ancient Mariner, Kubla Khan* and *Biographia Literaria.* Coleridge trekked from Nether Stowey in Somerset to drink to Kyrle's memory and to compose a Pope-ish ode to the dead benefactor.

In a letter to Robert Southey, dated July 13th, 1794, Coleridge wrote 'at Ross, we took our quarters up at the King's Arms, once the house of Kyrle, the Man of Ross. I gave the window-shutter the following effusion; Richer than Misers, etc'. Coleridge's poem *Ode to the Man of Ross,* which it is suggested he wrote in the Summer house in Kyrle's garden, was published in the *Cambridge Intelligencer,* September 27th, 1794. An inveterate re-worker and re-shaper of his work, Coleridge left several versions, some, six lines short of the original 20. A brief extract should suffice.

Here dwelt the 'Man of Ross!' O Trav'ller, hear,
Departed Merit claims a reverent tear!
Friend to the friendless, to the sick man health,
With gen'rous joy he view'd his modest wealth;
He heard the widow's heav'n-breath prayer of praise!
He mark'd the shelter'd orphan's tearful gaze!'

Coleridge ended the poem with a toast to Kyrle; *'Beneath this roof, if thy cheer'd moments pass, Fill to the Good Man's Name one grateful Glass!*

The graffiti Coleridge scratched on the 'window shutter' may have been accidentally erased long ago by an over zealous decorator, or window cleaner. The King's Arms passed through several hands, and was eventually purchased by John Stratford Collins, who had it converted into shops, and the stables and outbuildings into 'shambles'. These were joyously frequented by the public on market days, until the shambles were deemed to be interfering with the long and acquisitive claw of the Marquis of Bath, who owned the ancient manorial rights which included the tolls of Ross market. The shambles were immediately closed to the town's citizens, just as the cancelling of the corn tolls destroyed John Kyrle's free bread scheme for the hungry and destitute.

Across the road from Kyrle's house, the King's Head has been pouring ale and providing accommodation for travellers and horses since it opened its doors in 14th century. The pub, sadly now horse free, still thrives, providing vittles and ale in a tranquil, pleasantly old fashioned setting which Kyrle would surely have appreciated. Kyrle's affinity with the staff at the Nag's Head, not to mention the quality of cider, led to the formation of John Kyrle supporters club in the 1850s. In 1947 The Hereford Citizen reported 'in Ross, at the Nag's Head, we find a club named after this famous man in the 1850s - the John Kyrle or Man of Ross Lodge of Loyal and Independent Old Friends'. Also, at the New Inn, now the Eagle, appropriately on the corner of Kyrle Street, there was another Loyal Man of Ross Lodge, Manchester Unity. Both Lodges came into existence in 1853.

Portraits of Kyrle

John Kyrle was not lionised in his lifetime. In fact before Pope 'discovered' him, the Man of Ross was just that, a fellow from Ross, practically unknown outside the town. Before the days of the camera, people, local friends and admirers most probably wanted a painting of Kyrle, a sketch even. Kyrle is said to have resisted the strongest solicitations to sit for a portrait. Samuel Ireland pointed out that 'no inducement could prevail on him to comply with the request of his friends'. Charles Heath suggested that certain gentlemen of Ross took no notice of Kyrle's wishes and, without telling the subject, 'engaged an artist from London who sketched Kyrle while he sat at church, attending Divine Service on a Sunday'. To impudently invade the thoughts of a respected worshipper, without being summarily ejected, is a mystery of course. Kyrle, so aware of his own worth, may have arranged 'the sitting'.

The sly sketch of Kyrle, 'done under circumstances that ruled it against accuracy', spawned a series of copies. One ended up in the King's Arms, another hung in the King's Head. Mrs. Prosser, owner of the painting, said Kyrle was portrayed in a 'robe de chambre, his cravat hanging below his chest, after the fashion of King William III'. This was not exactly the sort of apparel Kyrle would wear at any time, let alone in church. 'The hair of his wig was parted at the top and combed down close to Kyrle's ears, below which it hung', trilled Mrs Prosser. 'Our modern beaux lately introduced such an imitation'. There was, 'something extremely calm and placid, in Kyrle's countenance, corresponding with his benevolent demeanour'. A trenchant observer declared that the 'poorly executed portrait of Kyrle at the King's Arms Inn, depicted a man close to death'.

When the Kings Arms landlord, George Wall, left Ross in 1795 for the Swan Inn in Tewkesbury, he took the painting of Kyrle with him, leaving the Kings Arms clientele, who had become attached to the picture, quite devastated. Sir Mark Sykes claimed he subsequently purchased the picture from Wall for 13 guineas, and hung it in his family home, Strettington Hall, near Malton. The portrait did not actually belong to Wall, the man who walked off with it, but to Stratford Collins. A third edition, belonging to Phillip Jones, surfaced. It was said to be of Kyrle as a young man of about 22 or 23, with handsome, clean, unworried good looks and luxuriant black hair flopping over his face. The painting was later dismissed by 'a connoisseur' as 'mere daubing'.

In the early twentieth century, an Indian ink sketch of the King's Arms Inn picture was discovered among papers belonging to Charles Heath, and was later sold to the late Rev. A.W. Chatfield of Much Marcle. On the back was written 'This drawing was made by the Rev. J. Gardner, of Christ's College, Cambridge, the artist who made the drawings for Mr. Cox's Historical Tour in Monmouthshire from the original at the King's Arms Ross, and was given to Charles Heath'. An oil portrait believed to be the original of this picture was in the possession of J.S. Fletcher, Esq., M.P. for Hampstead, whose intention was to donate it to the Tate Gallery.

The Man of Ross, by Josef Van Aken (1669-1749), described as 'probably the earliest representation in art of John Kyrle', was painted at least a decade after his death in 1724. According to Hilda F. Finberg, in her piece in the Burlington Magazine of September 1940, this has 'baffled elucidation'. The portrait of Kyrle, astride a fine grey horse against a picturesque background, though neither signed nor dated, is, says Finberg, 'unquestionably the work of one of the three Van Aken, or Van Haecken, brothers', probably Joseph, who painted portraits in England in the first half of the eighteenth century. Finberg asserts that the subject represents an incident taken from life, or from literature. Kyrle's eyes, she notes, 'are fixed on the boy running towards him, whose shabby clothes proclaim his poverty. The other boy, standing near the horse's head, wears a bright red jerkin and black apron, possibly the uniform of the charity school, to which Kyrle contributed during his lifetime. The lady wears a full-skirted sage green dress with blue bodice, large Leghorn hat underlined with pink and red sandals; the gentleman, who stands aloof, eyeing the artist, seems by his dark full bottomed wig, and suit of puce-coloured velvet, to belong to an earlier age'.

A portrait of Kyrle of some quality was painted by Sir Peter Lely (1618-1680). Born in Germany, of Dutch parents, Lely arrived in London in 1643 and became the dominant portrait painter at Court, succeeding Anthony Van Dyke as one of the most admired artists in England. Lely's portrait of the Man of Ross depicts a ruddy faced man in his mid thirties. Samuel Ireland included an etching of this portrait in his book, *Picturesque Views of the River Wye*, commenting 'I flatter myself the annexed etching from this picture will not prove unacceptable to the admirer and collector of portraits, as I do not remember to have ever seen a print of this exalted character'.

A talented and versatile painter, much of Lely's work was 'synonymous with a certain style of full-busted, fresh faced women showing plenty of cleavage'. Lely was a familiar figure in the Royal Court, becoming King Charles I favourite portraitist. After the King lost his head, Lely painted Oliver Cromwell and become Principal Painter in Ordinary to King Charles II. Lely's portraits hang in prestigious galleries and houses around the world, including Hampton Court Palace, Burghley House and the National Maritime Museum at Greenwich.

A portrait of Kyrle, copied from the original sketch, and numbered 83, hangs in the Balliol College library among a long, stern line of eminent Balliol students. The oil on canvas portrait, painted around 1720 when the man of Ross was 83, was given by Charles Septimus Money Kyrle to his godson and kinsman, RE Prothero, Baron Ernle, who attended Balliol in 1871, and who presented the painting of Kyrle to the College before 1925. It was described in the *Balliol College Portraits Catalogue* as 'early, possibly original'. A tablet on the frame records it as 'an Original Painting of John Kyrle ye Man of Ross'. The portrait reveals a pensive man with a cast in his left eye, wearing a long grey scarf, and gazing down. Kyrle looks unsure of himself among the bright and thrusting Balliol men and women, who after tossing their mortar boards to the skies, go out to change the world. Another portrait of Kyrle, one attributed to Sir Godfrey Kneller, depicting a handsome and boyish Kyrle with lustrous locks, was lent to the National Portrait Exhibition in South Kensington in 1867.

The Man of Ross Portioning a Bride was painted by Charles Lucy, a self taught but eminent Hereford artist, and Freeman of the city, in 1841. Lucy painted dramatic scenes from the lives of the famous, Oliver Cromwell, King Charles 1, Garibaldi, Lord Nelson and Lord Saye and Sele, who had once, 'traitorously corrupted the youth of England by setting up a grammar school'. The Kyrle painting, described as 'a charming work', originally belonged to a Hereford doctor, John Bleek or Bleeck-Lye, who lived in Castle Street. It passed to another Hereford citizen, a Mr. Cam. The last portrait by the ailing Lucy was to be of James Rankin of Bryngyn, High Sheriff of Hereford, founder of the Hereford Free Library and Museum, but the subject died aged fifty-nine before Lucy could start. The last remnant of Lucy's work in Hereford was a fresco he painted for St.Martin's Church, which unfortunately was erased when the church walls were scrubbed during renovation.

In 1987, Ross Town council discovered a portrait of Kyrle in their strong room. The canvas was described as in good condition in a slightly damaged gilt scrolled frame. A label with it read 'Portrait of John Kyrle, The man of Ross - Johan van der Banck, portrait painter, born in England, it is supposed, of Dutch parentage'. Van der Banck (1686-1739) painted numerous portraits, some of distinguished persons, including Alexander Pope. He was fashionable during the reigns of the early Georges, and was said to be superior to Hogarth. As he also sold copies of the great masters, Bancks's work is of limited interest and value today. He died of consumption in London.

Memorabilia

Among Kyrle's belongings when he died was a small statue of Ceres, the Goddess of agriculture and fertility, before whom, man, it is believed, lived like snuffling hogs, naked and dirty, rooting for fungi and what fruits and nuts fell off trees. An important Roman diety, Ceres was associated with bread and plenty, with ripe crops of waving corn, and the certainty of an abundant harvest. She was versatile and took care of fertilisation, ploughing and planting. She led walks through abundant fields at harvest time, and joined labourers and their families gathering in the harvest, and celebrated when the harvest was threshed and in the barns. She was a woman of the people who protected their laws and their rights. One can see how this admirable woman appealed to the Ross benefactor.

Kyrle's diary, which is said to have contained personal notes and thoughts, has, like much else associated with him, disappeared. He lent it to James Prosser, who carrying it about with him, either had it stolen or allowed it to slide from his pocket. Prosser suggested the cherished item might be among his mother's paper. It wasn't. Heath remarked that 'the observations of such a man as Mr. Kyrle, if made public, would have afforded much curiosity, and pleasant remark, in contrasting them with the manners of the present day.'

A chair, said to be 'quaint enough' to be one Kyrle sat on, made of oak and five feet two inches high, the pinnacle included, and two feet nine inches broad, was presented to a Mr. Newman, of the Ross Friendly Society after a local cabinet maker adorned the top with a 'circular moulding' bearing the society's name. Finding the chair an uncomfortable encumbrance, Newman had it thrown out, where it lay until someone decided to have it burnt. By some lucky chance, and on the insistence of stewards of the club, John Taynton and John Sharman, the chair survived and was offered to the parish

Detail from Kyrle's vault memorial, St Mary's Church ——

church where it remained in the chancel until the disbanding of the Ross Friendly Society, at which point it was sold and removed to the Kyrle Coffee House. The owners sold it in July 1897, for £23 to a Mr. Simmonds, 'a dealer in art treasures and curios' in Monmouth. Other chairs associated with the Man of Ross are the pair of sanctuary chairs in St.Mary's church. They are still there, heavy and handsome, with scrolled tops, carved backs, and what looks like intriguing punch marks on the arms. They date, it is believed, from the 17th century and were given to the church by Frederick Cooper, of Cooper and Preece, Ross, Stock Salesmen, Auctioneers, Rents, Debts and Tithes Collectors, Bailiffs, Timber Surveyors and, publishers of *The Kyrle*, a free register of properties for sale and let in the Wye Valley.

Kyrle's prayer book, with engraved silver plate, went to the late Mrs. A.J. Purchase of Chasedale, Ross, who also had an original autographed letter of Kyrle, and the Cubberly or Collins portrait of the Man of Ross, a replica of which was presented to the town by Mrs. A.W. Foster. An antique tea service of Kyrle's, and his original Will, were last seen in the possession of a Mrs. Powell Bennett of Phocle Green. A very fine silver medal, with a bust of John Kyrle and a graceful figure of Ceres, given as a prize in 1826 by the Ross Horticultural Society, eventually found its way to Frederick Cooper.

On June 25th, 1918, a party from the Woolhope Club visited Colonel Foster at Brockampton Court and were shown the Kyrle Room which housed legal deeds signed by him, an autographed letter in 'bold penmanship' and the Kyrle Family Bible. Visitors also inspected a portrait of Kyrle wrongly attributed to Sir Godfrey Kneller, as well as an 'exquisitely engrossed' copy of Pope's eulogy to the Man of Ross. Another item, indisputably once the property of the Man of Ross, was a small, mathematical treatise written by the Rev. John Newton and elaborately signed by Kyrle.

One of the more interesting recent finds associated with the Man of Ross, is a gold mourning ring. Probably never intended to be worn, mourning rings, usually gold, were given by the wealthy to

Lady Dupplin's memorial to John Kyrle, St Mary's Church ——

close friends to commemorate a dead relative, whose name and date of birth and death, with a legend or motto, were inscribed on it. The rings, which could number from half a dozen to several hundred, depending on the wealth and ego of the dead person, were paid for by him, or mentioned in his will along with a list of recipients. The weight and elegance of a mourning ring often depended on the social status of the receiver. John Kyrle's mourning ring has a small transparent, sealed locket on top, around which is etched 'The Man of Ross'. The inside of the ring is inscribed with Kyrle's name, his date of birth, unfortunately incorrectly, as the 26th, instead of the 22nd of May, and the Latin phrase, Virtute et Fide, (Virtue and Faith). The locket contains a tiny curl of silver hair, possibly snipped from the head of the Man of Ross after his death.

Two centuries after his death, Kyrle was still considered a potent weapon among local advertisers, with his name seen on hoardings, billboards, inns and street signs. The Man of Ross pub in Wye Street, built in the 1830s on the footprint of a 17th century building, was once the Man of Ross Inn - an eating house run by James Watkins, a corn merchant in 1847. John William Millington, 'a sign painter, and heraldic and scenic artist', took over the licence and re-named the pub, ye Man of Ross Inn. Currently being refurbished, it survives. The Man of Ross Weekly Newspaper was published in the 19th century by J W F Counsell and ran from 1855 to 1866. As well as advertising 'cures' for baldness, scabies and fatigue, it printed stories about gypsy picnics regularly held on Wormelow Tump, and the Annual Rook Shoot Dinner at the Harewood End Inn.

Kyrle's Coffee House started a coffee obsession in the town, which shows no sign of abating. Kyrle Cycles, built for Speed, Strength and Durability, were rolling off the production line. There were Kyrle boots, the John Kyrle Fire Engine, more of a handcart with a hand pump, the John Kyrle Football Club and the Crack Kyrle Cycle Race. The Grammar School was closed in 1979, and a brand new Comprehensive called the John Kyrle High School, now an Academy, opened.

The Man of Ross, a popular inn since 1847 ———

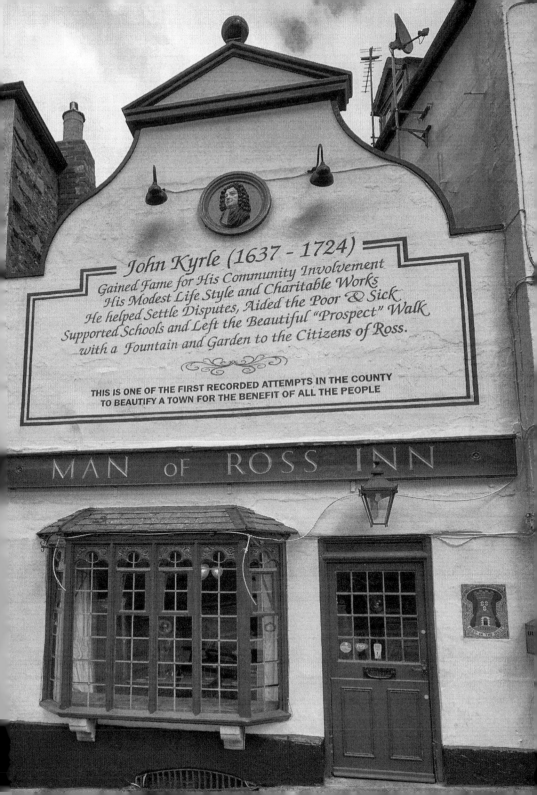

John Kyrle (1637 - 1724)
Gained Fame for His Community Involvement
His Modest Life Style and Charitable Works
He helped Settle Disputes, Aided the Poor & Sick
Supported Schools and Left the Beautiful "Prospect" Walk
with a Fountain and Garden to the Citizens of Ross.

THIS IS ONE OF THE FIRST RECORDED ATTEMPTS IN THE COUNTY
TO BEAUTIFY A TOWN FOR THE BENEFIT OF ALL THE PEOPLE

MAN of ROSS INN

Henry Dowell, whose sign boasted 'Under the Patronage of the Royal Family', built boats to order at Dock Pitch and had piles of scented timber maturing in the sun and rain. Dowell's workshop was abuzz with the sounds of sawing, the air full of sawdust and newly applied varnish. Dowell offered boat trips from Ross to Chepstow on board his 'safe, commodious, and elegantly fitted up steamboat called the Man of Ross, which he slid into the Wye, to great acclaim on Monday June 27th, 1836 and dreamily chugged to Chepstow and back twice weekly in summer. The Grand Opening of the Kyrle Picture Palace in 1913 was conducted by Colonel Middleton of the Chase, now a hotel, with Miss Wyatt all the way from Matlock on the piano. The Kyrle Picture Palace closed in 1950, and was demolished in the 1970s.

Kyrle's Legacy

Although it is for his major projects, the Causeway, the Prospect, the bringing of water to the town and the voracious tree planting, that Kyrle is famous, it was for his small charitable works in and around Ross, that he acquired the 'the Man of Ross' moniker. Even when he couldn't afford it, Kyrle dropped a few coins into young brides' trousseaux, helped finance the burying of paupers, and quietly assisted the bankrupt to regain respectability

While the world outside the market town of Ross churned and fomented, the modest, obscure and contented Kyrle planned projects for the local good. In this he achieved a great deal more than his wealthier friends. Instead of ignoring the hungry and the handicapped, the sick and the unlovable, Kyrle welcomed them into his house and encouraged them to linger by his fireside, even though he may have been worn out and ready for bed. Erskine-Hill summed

Mourning ring, with lock of Kyrle's hair (Jackson Collection)
Commemorative medallion c.1890 (Jackson Collection)
Kyrle family coat of arms
John Kyrle's seal (Hereford Record Office)

him up succinctly. 'Kyrle was 'a private individual with limited resources, fulfilling the traditional obligations of those born into a more affluent and public role in life. He saw the country house ideal fulfilled - without the country house'.

Kyrle had the Causeway repaired, lengthened and strengthened by ungloved men and their horses, without the assistance of pre-heated tarmac, ready mixed concrete, traffic lights and mechanical diggers. With little more it seems, than a magician's wave of his hand, he caused silvery water to gurgle from standpipes stationed at corners all over the town, ceasing for many the drudgery of twice daily trips to the well in rain and blizzard.

Fittingly, for a man ahead of his time, Kyrle is said to have re-built the greater part of the 14th century spire of Ross Church with recycled materials, largely at his own expense. It was certainly repaired in 1721, during Kyrle's lifetime, but there is no account in the Parish Register of his involvement. However, in *The Life of John Kyrle*, by Lawrence and Fowler, published in 1912, it is claimed that Kyrle called the meeting at which the decision was made to remove and re-build the mouldering and clearly dangerous spire. Kyrle is also said to have added four new 25 feet tall pinnacles to the corners of the tower. Unsurprisingly, his box pew, one of the oldest in the church, was spared when the others, rodent gnawed and worm eaten, were consigned to the bonfire during refurbishing.

With a little unobtrusive assistance from Thomas Blake, Kyrle's most visible and enduring gift to the town is the Prospect, with its bracing and classically English views of the river Wye, the plains, the noble skeleton of Wilton Castle and the cultivated slopes beyond. Kept manicured and litter free by Ross Council, the Prospect's lawns, trees and flowerbeds remain an essential amenity for locals and visitors alike. Sadly, and bewilderingly, the pleasant nature and bright and airy feel of the Prospect was rudely interrupted by archaeological excavations in 2009. This meant the felling of a mature and healthy sequoia, and the excavation of an increasingly

Route of the John Kyrle Walk today (Hereford Council) ——

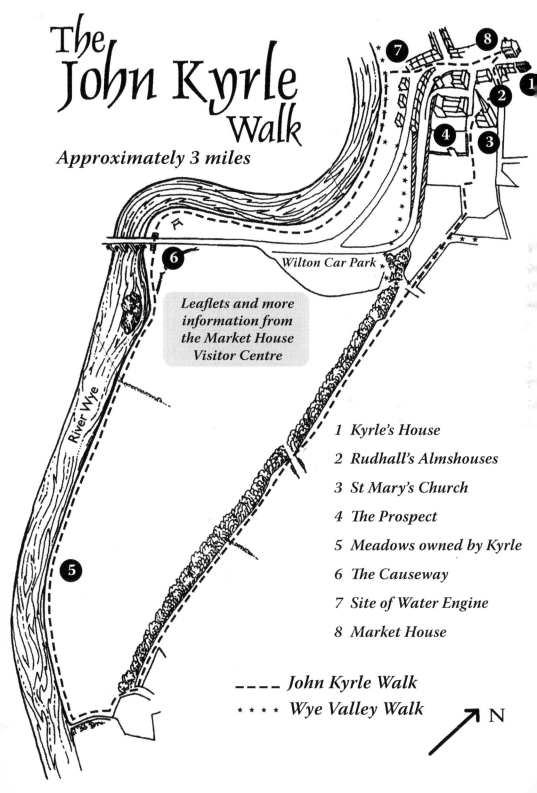

The John Kyrle Walk

Approximately 3 miles

Leaflets and more information from the Market House Visitor Centre

Wilton Car Park

River Wye

1 Kyrle's House
2 Rudhall's Almshouses
3 St Mary's Church
4 The Prospect
5 Meadows owned by Kyrle
6 The Causeway
7 Site of Water Engine
8 Market House

- - - - John Kyrle Walk
★ ★ ★ ★ Wye Valley Walk

N

large hole. Rain came, plastic flapped, there were months of muddy inconvenience. The dig eventually revealed the usual Time Team detritus, old coins, trading tokens, flints, ceramic, with the addition of the skeleton of a horse, which the contractors suggested might have a Roman connection. After much speculation, followed by a long and continuing silence, the company who did the work have been singularly unforthcoming about their actual 'finds', much to the chagrin of simmering Ross ratepayers. Despite riots, trespass, vandalism and one optimistic speculator who stood on the Prospect a century ago, rubbing his be-ringed hands and gloating that 'this will present a very desirable spot for the erection of villas which would form an important improvement to the town', the Prospect survives as a beloved public amenity for every citizen and visitor to Ross to enjoy. Exactly what the Man of Ross envisaged.

The John Kyrle walk, beginning at the benefactor's monogrammed gate on the south side of the Prospect, was Kyrle's favourite stroll, and on old maps it is framed by tall elms planted by him and his devoted labourers. For many a year, in sunshine and in snow, Kyrle purposefully strode to his Summer house for peaceful reflection after work, before heading back to the town, with St. Mary's elegant spire beckoning in the distance. As he aged, Kyrle continued to walk, now cautiously picking his steps, his stick saluting gleaners and farmers as they toiled. For three centuries thousands of Rossians, their children and their canines, have gambolled and ambled along this winding stretch above the river, studying wildlife, or chasing butterflies, conscious perhaps, of the bells of St.Mary's tolling across the fields. The once spectacular views looking west along the walk are all but obliterated by dense bushes in urgent need of a trim. Mapped and signed, the John Kyrle walk now takes an optional detour to the venerable Wilton Bridge, and one of the riverside inns for a refreshing cider before heading back to the town.

The Kyrle Society and The National Trust

It is not widely known that Kyrle played a significant role in the foundation of the National Trust. Octavia Hill (1838-1912), an inspired social reformer and staunch believer in Kyrle's ideals, was co-founder with her sister Miranda of the Society for the Diffusion of Beauty in 1876, which later devolved into the John Kyrle Society. The stated aim of the Society was 'to bring the refining and cheering influences of natural and artistic beauty home to the people and to promote gardening among the industrious classes'.

The dynamic Octavia Hill extolled the virtues and claims of the Kyrle Society. She spoke proudly of the Society's success in providing open spaces and libraries for the public, posting books to deprived readers, not just all over England 'but to the Shetland Islands, the West Indies, and even to Australia'. The Kyrle Society organised 'oratorios and concerts' which gave pleasure to thousands, while her 'decorative branch, transformed numerous bare and ugly parish halls, club rooms and similar institutions into bright, artistic, and pleasant places of rest and recreation'. The Kyrle Society was one of the many mentioned in Glasgow University's *Exhibition Culture in Nineteenth Century London 1878-1908*, which recorded smaller and less well known societies as well as commercial and artist led exhibitions in major institutions such as the Royal Academy and the Grosvenor Gallery. The University website database documents over 3,000 exhibitions and 900 galleries in London galleries between 1878 and 1908. The entry on the Kyrle Society states that 'it was to bring the refining and cheering influences of natural and artistic beauty home to the people; this it purposes to effect by decorating Workmen's Clubs, Hospitals, and Schools'.

A Bristol branch was founded in 1905, getting straight down to business and sticking loyally to the Man of Ross's original template: preserving historic and beautiful buildings; discouraging dull, mean, and monotonous building; improving waste spaces by planting trees and shrubs, providing seats, and encouraging the cultivation of flowers in yards and small gardens, in window boxes, on tops of walls, on railway cuttings and embankments; persuading schools, clubs and other organisations to preserve wildlife. For near forty years the Bristol John Kyrle Society played its part in civic affairs, until it was subsumed by a new society with an extended field of activity and wider aims covering the whole of the City and its neighbourhood'. At a special General Meeting of the Kyrle Society on June 8th, 1943, John Kyrle's name disappeared from the headed note paper, but his beliefs still influence the Bristol Civic Society.

The indomitable Miss Hill worked tirelessly for over half a century towards her vision of a socially inclusive society, 'for ever, for everyone'. Well ahead of the politicians of her time, Hill demonstrated how access to the arts and beauty could help heal what Benjamin Disraeli prophetically called, the 'two nations' class divide. Lives of the poor were blighted, not simply by poverty, but also by ignorance and ugliness. The dogged way Kyrle battled to lease, beautify and protect the Prospect for everyone was echoed later by Hill's successful efforts to fight off developers and save Parliament Hill Fields in London. Hill also campaigned for a Commons Preservation Society, and had footpaths added, saying, they were 'one of the greatest common inheritances to which English citizens are born'.

With others, Octavia Hill formed the National Trust for places of Historic Interest or Natural Beauty, which led to the founding of the National Trust in 1895. The Octavia Hill Museum in Wisbech boasts many tributes to the Man of Ross, including a stained glass window commemorating the works of the Kyrle Society, with a mural depicting images of people whose ideas were central to the Trust's founding. They include, John Ruskin, Thomas Carlyle and John Kyrle.

After 300 years, Kyrle's philosophy of helping the poor continues through the Community Larder. Run as in Kyrle's time, by a combination of generous citizens and volunteers from Ross

Churches, donations of non-perishable foods are fittingly received at St. Mary's Church Hall, which arose from the ruins of the Grammar School which John Kyrle helped to establish.

Thus ends an attempt to put flesh on the bones, and insert blood into the dried up veins of the elusive, compassionate, John Kyrle, who in spite of his naysayers, will be always be remembered and revered as, The Man of Ross.

Bibliography

Excursion Down the Wye, 1799, Charles Heath, (Monmouth Museum)

Excursion Down the Wye, 1803, Charles Heath, (Monmouth Museum)

Excursion Down the Wye, 1828, Charles Heath, (Hurley Collection)

The Story of Ross, 1999, Dr. Pat Hughes and Heather Hurley

Hereford & Tintern Cathedrals, Abbeys and Famous Churches, 1925, Edward Foord

The Book of Ross-on-Wye, 1980, Martin H.Morris

The Wye Tour, 1896, compiled and written by J.A. Stratford

Picturesque View of the River Wye, 1797, Samuel Ireland

Personalities of the Forest of Dean, 1883, Rev. H.G.Nicholls, (Fineleaf Editions, 2007)

History, Topography and Directory of Herefordshire, 1858, Edward Cassey and Co.

Littlebury's Directory and Gazateer of the County of Hereford, 1867

Material on the various Ross Charities, Ross Rectory Box, Hereford Record Office

A Survey of Historic Parks & Gardens in Herefordshire, 2001, David Whitehead

Royal Commission on Historical Monuments, England - Herefordshire, 1932

Report of the Commissioners Concerning Charities, 1819-1837

The Local Historian's Encyclopaedia, 1898, John Richardson

History of the Mansions and Manors of Herefordshire, 1872, Rev. Charles J. Robinson

Ancient Woodlands and Trees of Herefordshire, Our Heritage Revealed, 2006-2009

Memorial of the Civil War in Herefordshire, 1879, Reverend John Webb

The Civil War in Hereford, 1995, Ron Shoesmith

The Story of Bill Mills, 2001, Heather Hurley

Voltaire, Histoire de Jenni, 1775

Victoria County History - Gloucestershire

Wilton Castle and Wilton Bridge, 1884, Rev. H. Tweed

John Kyrle, philanthropist and landscape designer, David Whitehead, Oxford Dictionary of National Biography

John Newton (1621-1678), Mathematician, Oxford Dictionary of National Biography

The Beautiful Works of the Reverend Mr. Stephen Duck, 1753

A Good Plain Country Town, Ross on Wye, 1800-1930, 1980, Fred Druce

Kings and Queens of England and Great Britain, 1966, Eric R Delderfield

The Book of Ledbury, 1982, Joe Hillaby
Old Humphrey's Country Strolls, 1844, George Mogridge
The Buildings of England: Herefordshire, 1963, Nikolaus Pevsner
The Book of South Wales, the Wye and the Coast, 1861, S.C. and A.M Hall
The Wye Tour and its Artists, 2010, Julian Mitchell
Water-mills of the Monnow & Trothy 1976, SD Coates and DG Tucker
The Pubs of Ross and South Herefordshire, 2001, Heather Hurley
Alexander Pope, 1880, Sir Leslie Stephen
Alexander Pope, a Life, 1985, Maynard Mack
The Works of Alexander Pope, Esq. 1764
The Social Milieu of Alexander Pope, 1975, Howard Erskine-Hill
Alexander Pope, The Poet and the Landscape, 1999, Mavis Batey
The Alexander Pope Encyclopaedia, 1938, Pat Rogers
A Ross Anthology, Quotations Spanning a Thousand Years, 1999, Jon Hurley
Ross on Wye, a photographic History, 2002, Heather Hurley
Saints and Sinners of the Marches, 2012, Michael Tavinor
Thomas Hearne, Remarks & Collections, C.E.Doble & D.W.Rannie
The Picturesque Landscape, 1994, S. Daniels & C.Watkins
Beauties of England & Wales Vol. V, 1805, Edward Wedlake Brayley & John Britton
Wanderings and Excursion in South Wales, 1837, Thomas Roscoe
Observations of the River Wye, 1770, William Gilpin, M.A.
A History of the Castles of Herefordshire, and their Lords, 1869, Rev. Charles J.Robinson (Logaston 2002) Narrative of a Pedestrian Ramble, 1839, Leith Ritchie
An Historical Account of the City of Hereford, 1796, John Price
The Life of John Kyrle, the Man of Ross, 1912, Lawrence and Fowler
Herefordshire Maps, 1577 to 1800, 2004, Brian Smith
A Treasured Inheritance, 600 years of Oxford College Silver, 2004, Helen M. Clifford
Kyrle's Relics at Brockhampton Court , (Woolhope Transactions), 1918
The Picturesque Landscape, Visions of Georgian Herefordshire, 1994, Stephen Daniels
Brief Memoir of John Kyrle, Esq., The Ross Guide, 1827
The Story of Herefordshire's Hospitals, 1999, Charles Renton
Herefordia, 1861, James Henry James
Holme Lacy House (Woolhope Transactions), 2011, David Whitehead
Ross Parish Church, (Woolhope Transactions), 1918, Rev. R.T.A. Money-Kyrle
Doomsday Book entries for the district around Ross-on-Wye (Historical Aspects of Ross), Ross Civic Society, 2010, Ian Standing

Reflections of Ross on Wye, 1973, M.H. Morris

Foy Parish Records, BN 88/1, Hereford Record Office

Collection towards the History and Antiquities of the County of Hereford, 1922, John Hobson Herefordshire Militia Assessments of 1663, 1972, Ed. M.A. Faraday

History and Antiquities of the County of Hereford, 1882, W.H. Cooke

Diocese of Hereford Institutions, etc., (AD 1539-1900), 1923, Ed. A.T. Bannister

The Poetry of Allusion, 1968, Reuben A.Brower

Ross Parish Records, 1821, Thomas Jenkins, Hereford Record Office

The Gateway of the Wye Valley, 1945, Ross on Wye, Chamber of Commerce

Burrow's Guide to the Wye, 1930

Holiday in the Wye Valley and the Royal Forest of Dean, 1939, Jakemans Ltd

Historic Aspects of Ross, Vol. 1, 2000, Ross on Wye Civic Society

Octavia Hill, 1833-1912, 2012, Peter Clayton

Mediaeval Chantries, 1963, G.H. Cooke

A Boke of Gode Cookery (Woolhope Transactions), 1997, James L. Matterer

Articles, Pamphlets, Documents and Maps

Death of Walter Kyle, father of the Man of Ross, Collection at Longleat

A true and perfect Inventory of the Goods Chattles and Cattles of Alice Kyrle, of Rosse, in the County of Hereford Widdow deceased taken and apprised the third day of Aprill one Thousand six Hundred sixty three: by us whose names are underwritten. Transcribed from the original by Dr. Pat Hughes. (Heather Hurley Collection)

IV Cuttings p.158, Hereford Reference Library, Local Collection 942.44

News Letter, November 19th 1724, -Bodl. Rawl. MSS. 151, fol.198

Minutes of the Society of Commissioners of Charitable Associations of Ross, 1675-76, Hereford Record Office F44/1.

Ross Gazette, July 9th 1925, AA1 a 46/14/2, Hereford Record Office

Report of the Commissioners for Hereford Charities, 1819/37, Hereford Record Office

Assignment of lease, Viscount Weymouth, John Kyrle, William Fisher and others, G87/33/5, Gloucester Record Office

Herefordshire Journal, August 29th 1798, William Dobbs' Obituary, Hereford Ref. Lib.

Ross Gazette, April 16th 1987, article on John Kyrle's portraits by Martin Morris

Ross Gazette May 21st 1987, article on John Kyrle, by Martin Morris

Thomas Webbe's Will, 1612, partly transcribed by Sue Hubbard, TNA, 11/124

Reginae Elizabethe. Chap. xxiiij. An Act for the erecting and building of a bridge

ouer the Riuer Wie at Wilton on Wie, Rosse, in the Countie of Hereford, 1597
The Man of Ross Weekly, July, 1855.
The Saturday Magazine, Supplement for October, 1832, The Man of Ross.
Royal Hotel printed deeds and documents, circa 1955. Heather Hurley Collection
Pilgrimages to English Shrines, 1853, Anna Marie Hall & F.C. Fairholt
Pilgrimage to the Tomb of John Kyrle, 1853, Mrs. S.C. Hall, Hereford Reference Lib
Thomas Blake, 1825-1901, the Pious Benefactor, 1996, Jon Hurley, Ross Civic Society
River Crossings at Wilton-on-Wye, 2000, Historical Aspects of Ross, Heather Hurley
Hereford Hearth Tax, 1665
Ross Parish Boundaries, Paper by the Rev. Hill, 1646, RRC11 BW 14/42 1747
Ross Charity School Accounts Book, 1709, Hereford Records Office, Ref., BW14/97
Cassini Old Series Historical Maps, 1828-1831
Observations on the Present State of Ross, Vols. I and 11, 1827, John Hall
Walter Kyrle: entry from J. Forster's Alumni Oxonienses
The Saturday Magazine, Vol.1, October 27th 1832
Boundaries of Ross, Hereford Record Office BG 99/1/15
The Man of Ross and the Kyrle Family, letter from T.C. Noble to the Editor of the Brighton Herald, 1882
Document relating to land at Dymock which Kyrle leased to Thomas Murrel, tailor. 1709, Gloucester Archives, D2957/116/11
Article in the Hereford Times, April 22nd 1933, regarding a contemporary copy of a term of agreement concerning the inequality of taxes paid by Ross Town and Ross Foreign in 1674, with John Kyrle as Umpire
The Blarney of John Kyrle. Pope's Humbug Exposed, Hereford Journal April 9th 1927
Medicines Advertised in Eighteenth-Century Bath newspapers, by P.S. Brown
Origins and Growth of the Dispensary Movement in England, 2003, I.S.L. Loudon
Hall's Observation on the Present State of Ross, Vols. 1 and 11, 1827, John Hall
Bluecoat Charity School, Ross, Hereford Record Office W/14/97
Petty Constables Returns 1656, Longleat Library, accounts and correspondence 1707
Burials in the Churchyard of Ross from 1670, Hereford Record Office BW 14/140
The King of Good Neighbours, Parish Magazine, November, 1893, Jennett Humphreys
The Church of St. Mary-the-Virgin, Ross, c. 1950, Rev. E.H. Beattie
T 52, Capital messuage called Over Ross, or the Old House, manorial admission of John Kyrle, 1694, G87/33/5, Assignment of Lease, 6 of Sep. 1705
Births, Marriages and Burials in Ross, Parish Records on microfiche, Hereford ROff
Changing Faces of Herefordshire's Many Courts, 2001, V. Watts

D4762/11, Award of umpire Jn. Kyrle, Town and Forren, 1674, Hereford Archives

K2/11/64, Deed to Lead Uses of a Fine, 1st of June, 1689, Hereford Archives

K2 /11/65, Lease, (1) Elizabeth Kyrle of Walford, Spinster, (2) John Kyrle of Rosse, Esq. and William Gwillym Snr. Of Langstone, Hereford Archives

Articles of Marriage, (1) Robert Yate of Bristol, (2) Sir Edward Harley of Brampton Castle, John Kyrle of Ross, Sir William Merrick, knight, Thomas Scroope and Robert Henley, merchants all, of Bristol. And (3), Mary Kyrle of Walford, Hereford Archives, K2 /11/66

Quit Claim, 20th of June, 1690, with Consideration of parties who have entered into bonds of £200 for payments £10 p.a., to John Kyrle of Ross, Esq. to be paid to Robert Kyrle, eldest son of Sir Richard Kyrle of Ireland, Kt., deceased, Hereford Archives, K2/11/67

John Venn and the Hereford Society for Aiding the Industrious, 1988, Jean O'Donnell, Woolhope Transactions Vol. XLV1

Upton Bishop, Lease for a Year 4th of May, 1713, (1) William Collins and Mary his wife. (2) John Kyrle of Ross esq. and James Collins, gent., Hill Court Walford, Record of the Estate of the Clarke family, Hereford Record Office F8 /11/184

Pilley Collection (Photographic Collection), 914.244, Hereford Reference Library

Vicars Choral Endowment, REF 3779 (Leases relating to John Kyrle of Ross and John Hereford of Holme Lacy), Hereford County Archives

Abrahall,, concerning Ross on Wye and John, Viscount Scudamore, Bennett Hoskins of Harewood, Sir John Hoskins, son of Bennett Hoskins, John Newton, rector (sic) of Ross, John Kyrle and many others, Ref. 4686 Charities, Hereford County Archives

The History of Parliament, British, Political, Social and Local History-background to Col. Jeremiah Bubb's election as Governor of Carlisle on the 3rd of March, 1690, Harewood End Agricultural Society Archive

The Bristol Civic Society, Incorporating the Bristol John Kyrle Society, The First Sixty Years, 1905-1965, Vincent Waite

Exhibition Culture in London, 1878-1908, Dr. Joanna Meacock 2006, Glasgow Univ.

Prob. 11/247 choir 29 pp.223.R-224R of 1675 in PRO, Chancery Lane.

Will dated 16.9.1681 of Giles Winter of St. Sepulchre's without Newgate London [PROB 11/369 choir 27 p.214R-215RI of 1682 PRO, Chancery Lane

Websites

anglicanhistory.org

Ross-on-Wye.com

freepages.genealogy.rootsweb.ancestry.com

fineleaf